GW01605657

THE POET'S SPHERE

AN ANTHOLOGY OF ENGLISH VERSE

THE POET'S SPHERE

An Anthology of English Verse

Compiled by

C. F. BRICKNELL SMITH

Illustrated by David Harris

"Behold at last the poet's sphere!
But who," I said, "suffices here?
For, oh! so much he has to do;
Be painter and musician too!
The aspect of the moment show,
The feeling of the moment know."

Matthew Arnold

WHEATON

A Division of Pergamon Press

The Poet's Sphere

First published 1969
Reprinted 1974, 1975, 1978

Printed and bound in Great Britain by A. Wheaton & Co. Ltd, Exeter

ISBN 0 08 008737 x School edition
0 08 008853 8 Library edition

CONTENTS

1 Spring and Summer

2 Autumn and Winter

3 Country Life

4 The Countryside

5 Animals

6 Birds

7 Travel

8 The Sea

9 Laughter

10 Pleasures

12 Love—Its Problems

13 War

14 Morals

15 The Life of Man

16 Death

PREFACE

This anthology aims at providing a comprehensive introductory selection of short poems for the general reader and for appreciation classes in secondary and further education.

The poems are arranged to reveal some of the similarities and contrasts, in feeling, thought, form and diction, that distinguish different writers and different ages. They are, therefore, grouped into sections instead of being set in chronological or alphabetical order—although obviously the divisions cannot be rigid and many poems might claim a place in more than one category.

My sincere thanks are due to many friends and colleagues for their advice and comments, notably to Laurence Adkins, Cyril Poster and Dennis Kelland. I must accept the blame if I have not always followed their advice.

C.F.B.S.

What every poet starts from is his own emotions.

T. S. Eliot

1 Thaw

Over the land freckled with snow half-thawed
The speculating rooks at their nests cawed
And saw from elm-tops, delicate as flower of grass,
What we below could not see, Winter pass.

EDWARD THOMAS

2 Last Snow

Although the snow still lingers,
Heaped on the ivy's blunt webbed fingers
And painting tree-trunks on one side,
Here in this unlit ride
The fresh unchristened things appear,
Leaf, spathe and stem,
With crumbs of earth clinging to them
To show the way they came
But no flower yet to tell their name,
And one green spear,
Stabbing a dead leaf from below,
Kills winter at a blow.

ANDREW YOUNG

3 First Sight of Spring

The hazel-blooms, in threads of crimson hue,
Peep through the swelling buds, foretelling spring,
Ere a white-thorn leaf appears in view,
Or March finds throstles pleased enough to sing.
To the old touchwood tree woodpeckers cling
A moment, and their harsh-toned notes renew;
In happier mood, the stockdove claps his wing;
The squirrel sputters up the powdered oak,
With tail cocked o'er his head, and ears erect,
Startled to hear the woodman's understroke;
And with the courage which his fears collect,
He hisses fierce half malice and half glee
Leaping from branch to branch about the tree,
In winter's foliage, moss and lichens, decked.

JOHN CLARE

4 The Spring

Now that the Winter's gone, the earth hath lost
Her snow-white robes; and now no more the frost
Candies the grass, or casts an icy cream
Upon the silver lake or crystal stream:
But the warm sun thaws the benumbed earth,
And makes it tender, gives a sacred birth
To the dead swallow; wakes in hollow tree
The drowsy cuckoo and the humble bee.
Now do a quire of chirping minstrels bring
In triumph to the world, the youthful spring.

THOMAS CAREW

5 Night of Spring

Slow, horses, slow,
As through the woods we go –
We would count the stars in heaven,
Hear the grasses grow:

Watch the cloudlets few
Dappling the deep blue,
In our open palms outspread
Catch the blessed dew.

Slow, horses, slow,
As through the woods we go –
We would see fair Dian rise
With her huntress bow:

We would hear the breeze
Ruffling the dim trees,
Hear its sweet love-ditty set
To endless harmonies.

Slow, horses, slow,
As through the woods we go –
All the beauty of the night
We would learn and know!

THOMAS WESTWOOD

6 April Day: Binsey

Now the year's let loose; it skips like a feckless child,
Ruffles your hair, rouses the trees, runs wild,
Kisses the hills with sunlight, whips them with rain,
Tears the grass in passing, gets lost in the lane.
Taut as lyre-strings the swans' wings quiver,
Lyre-strings plucked by the wind on the swollen river.
Shadow of cloud and cantering horses race
Over the meadows where heaven and earth embrace.

MICHAEL HAMBURGER

7 Now the Full-Throated Daffodils

Now the full-throated daffodils,
Our trumpeters in gold,
Call resurrection from the ground
And bid the year be bold.

To-day the almond-tree turns pink,
The first flush of the spring;
Winds loll and gossip through the town
Her secret whispering.

Now too the bird must try his voice
Upon the morning air;
Down drowsy avenues he cries
A novel great affair.

He tells of royalty to be;
How with her train of rose,
Summer to coronation comes
Through waving wild hedgerows.

To-day crowds quicken in a street,
The fish leaps in the flood:
Look there, gasometer rises,
And here bough swells to bud.

For our love's luck, our stowaway,
Stretches in his cabin;
Our youngster joy barely conceived
Shows up beneath the skin.

Our joy was but a gusty thing
Without sinew or wit,
An infant flyaway; but now
We make a man of it.

C. DAY LEWIS

8 Spring Goeth All in White

Spring goeth all in white,
Crowned with milk-white may:
In fleecy flocks of light
O'er heaven the white clouds stray:

White butterflies in the air;
White daisies prank the ground:
The cherry and hoary pear
Scatter their snow around.

ROBERT BRIDGES

9 Spring

Nothing is so beautiful as spring –
  When weeds, in wheels, shoot long and lovely and
    lush:
  Thrush's eggs look little low heavens, and thrush
Through echoing timber does so rinse and wring
The ear, it strikes like lightnings to hear him sing;
  The glassy peartree leaves and blooms, they brush
  The descending blue; that blue is all in a rush
With richness; the racing lambs too have fair their fling.

What is all this juice and all this joy?
  A strain of the earth's sweet being in the beginning
In Eden garden. – Have, get, before it cloy,
  Before it cloud, Christ, lord, and sour with sinning,
Innocent mind and Mayday in girl and boy,
  Most, O maid's child, thy choice and worthy the
    winning.

GERARD MANLEY HOPKINS

10 **April Rise**

If ever I saw blessing in the air
I see it now in this still early day
Where lemon-green the vaporous morning drips
Wet sunlight on the powder of my eye.

Blown bubble-film of blue, the sky wraps round
Weeds of warm light whose every root and rod
Splutters with soapy green, and all the world
Sweats with the bead of summer in its bud.

If ever I heard blessing it is there
Where birds in trees that shoals and shadows are
Splash with their hidden wings and drops of sound
Break on my ears their crests of throbbing air.

Pure in the haze the emerald sun dilates,
The lips of sparrows milk the mossy stones,
While white as water by the lake a girl
Swims her green hand among the gathered swans.

Now, as the almond burns its smoking wick,
Dropping small flames to light the candled grass;
Now, as my low blood scales its second chance,
If ever world were blessed, now it is.

LAURIE LEE

11 **To Spring**

O thou with dewy locks, who lookest down
Through the clear windows of the morning, turn
Thine angel eyes upon our western isle,
Which in full choir hails thy approach, O Spring!

The hills tell each other, and the list'ning
Valleys hear; all our longing eyes are turned
Up to thy bright pavilions; issue forth,
And let thy holy feet visit our clime!

Come o'er the eastern hills, and let our winds
Kiss thy perfumèd garments; let us taste
Thy morn and evening breath; scatter thy pearls
Upon our love-sick land that mourns for thee.

O deck her forth with thy fair fingers; pour
Thy soft kisses on her bosom; and put
Thy golden crown upon her languished head,
Whose modest tresses were bound up for thee!

WILLIAM BLAKE

12 Home-Thoughts, from Abroad

O to be in England now that April's there,
And whoever wakes in England sees, some morning,
unaware,
That the lowest boughs and the brushwood sheaf
Round the elm-tree bole are in tiny leaf,
While the chaffinch sings on the orchard bough
In England – now!

And after April, when May follows,
And the whitethroat builds, and all the swallows!
Hark, where my blossomed pear-tree in the hedge
Leans to the field and scatters on the clover
Blossoms and dewdrops – at the bent spray's edge –
That's the wise thrush; he sings each song twice over,
Lest you should think he never could recapture
The first fine careless rapture!
And though the fields look rough with hoary dew,
All will be gay when noontide wakes anew
The buttercups, the little children's dower
– Far brighter than this gaudy melon-flower!

ROBERT BROWNING

13 **Song on May Morning**

Now the bright morning star, day's harbinger,
Comes dancing from the east, and leads with her
The flowery May, who from her green lap throws
The yellow cowslip, and the pale primrose.
  Hail, bounteous May, that dost inspire
  Mirth and youth and warm desire;
  Woods and groves are of thy dressing,
  Hill and dale doth boast thy blessing.
Thus we salute thee with our early song,
And welcome thee, and wish thee long.

JOHN MILTON

14 Summer

Winter is cold-hearted,
  Spring is yea and nay,
Autumn is a weathercock
  Blown every way:
Summer days for me
When every leaf is on its tree;

When Robin's not a beggar,
  And Jenny Wren's a bride,
And larks hang singing, singing, singing,
  Over the wheat-fields wide,
  And anchored lilies ride,
And the pendulum spider
  Swings from side to side;

And blue-black beetles transact business,
  And gnats fly in a host,
And furry caterpillars hasten
  That no time be lost,
And moths grow fat and thrive,
And ladybirds arrive.

Before green apples blush,
  Before green nuts embrown,
Why, one day in the country
  Is worth a month in town;
  Is worth a day and a year
Of the dusty, musty, lag-last fashion
  That days drone elsewhere.

CHRISTINA ROSSETTI

15 **Summer Night**

As we walk, the moon ahead of us
Appears to be falling through
Each tree we pass, and sieves
Star after star through screens
Of thickening leaves.

The green hedge is wider now
With white may, hanging grass. The chestnut
Trims itself with pink and snowy cones;
The moon as we walk drops through each tree
And scatters silvery grit among the country stones.

JAMES KIRKUP

16 Day of These Days

Such a morning it is when love
leans through geranium windows
and calls with a cockerel's tongue.

When red-haired girls scamper like roses
over the rain-green grass,
and the sun drips honey.

When hedgerows grow venerable,
berries dry black as blood,
and holes suck in their bees.

Such a morning it is when mice
run whispering from the church,
dragging dropped ears of harvest.

When the partridge draws back his spring
and shoots like a buzzing arrow
over grained and mahogany fields.

When no table is bare
and no bread dry
and the tramp feeds off ribs of rabbit.

Such a day it is when time
piles up the hills like pumpkins,
and the streams run golden.

When all men smell good,
and the cheeks of girls
are as baked bread to the mouth.

As bread and bean flowers
the touch of their lips,
and their white teeth sweeter than cucumbers.

LAURIE LEE

17 **Windy Day in August**

Over the vale, the sunburnt fields
A wind from the sea like a streamer unreels:
Dust leaps up, apples thud down,
The river's caught between a smile and a frown.

An inn-sign swinging, swinging to the wind,
Whines and whinges like a dog confined,
Round his paddock gallops the colt,
Dinghies at moorings curvet and jolt.

Sunlight and shadow in the copse play tig,
While the wallowing clouds talk big
About their travels, and thistle-down blows
Ghosting above the rank hedgerows.

Cornfield, orchard and fernland hail
Each other, waving from hill to hill:
They change their colours from morn to night
In play with the lissom, engaging light.

The wind roars endlessly past my ears,
Racing my heart as in earlier years.
Here and everywhere, then and now
Earth moves like a wanton, breathes like a vow.

C. DAY LEWIS

18 The Last Rose of Summer

'Tis the last rose of summer left blooming alone,
All her lovely companions are faded and gone.
No flower of her kindred, no rosebud is nigh
To reflect back her blushes or give sigh for sigh.

I'll not leave thee, thou lone one, to pine on the stem;
Since the lovely are sleeping, go sleep thou with them:
Thus kindly I scatter thy leaves o'er the bed
Where thy mates of the garden lie scentless and dead.

So soon may I follow when friendships decay,
And from love's shining circle the gems drop away.
When true hearts lie withered and fond ones are flown,
O who would inhabit this bleak world alone?

THOMAS MOORE

Poetry may be defined as a way of remembering what it would impoverish us to forget.

Robert Frost

19 **Autumn**

I love the fitful gust that shakes
  The casement all the day,
And from the glossy elm-tree takes
  The faded leaves away,
Twirling them by the window pane
With thousand others down the lane.

I love to see the shaking twig
  Dance till the shut of eve,
The sparrow on the cottage rig,
  Whose chirp would make believe
That Spring was just now flirting by
In Summer's lap with flowers to lie.

I love to see the cottage smoke
  Curl upwards through the trees,
The pigeons nestled round the cote
  On November days like these;
The cock upon the dunghill crowing,
The mill sails on the heath a-going.

The feather from the raven's breast
  Falls upon the stubble lea,
The acorns near the old crow's nest
  Drop pattering down the tree;
The grunting pigs, that wait for all,
Scramble and hurry where they fall.

JOHN CLARE

20 **Field of Autumn**

Slow moves the acid breath of noon
over the copper-coated hill,
slow from the wild crab's bearded breast
the palsied apples fall.

Like coloured smoke the day hangs fire,
taking the village without sound;
the vulture-headed sun lies low
chained to the violet ground.

The horse upon the rocky height
rolls all the valley in his eye,
but dares not raise his foot or move
his shoulders from the fly.

The sheep, snail-backed against the wall,
lifts her blind face but does not know
the cry her blackened tongue gives forth
is the first bleat of snow.

Each bird and stone, each roof and well,
feels the gold foot of autumn pass;
each spider binds with glittering snare
the splintered bones of grass.

Slow moves the hour that sucks our life,
slow drops the late wasp from the flower,
the rose tree's thread of scent draws thin –
and snaps upon the air.

LAURIE LEE

21 Last Leaves

Late last night, the moon in puddles, I walked the lane
North from my gate up to the small wood where,
Stirring and trembling from the sentient trees,
The last leaves fell. I heard them in the still air
Snap. And almost saw their sifting passage down
To join their squelching fellows on the ground,
All glory gone. I tread on the black wreck
Of the year. Well, it is over.
Here, in full arboreal Summer, struck
By the squinting light, I took for a hawk
No more than a flapping pigeon. I'll not make
That mistake in valid winter. No, I'll see
Each full-eyed owl stir not a breath
Of frost among the visible twigs as he pads
On air; and remember the owl's truth
For the vole, the silver frog, and the
Soft-bellied mouse, her Summer breeding done.

LESLIE NORRIS

22 Fall, Leaves, Fall

Fall, leaves, fall; die, flowers, away;
Lengthen night and shorten day;
Every leaf speaks bliss to me
Fluttering from the autumn tree.
I shall smile when wreaths of snow
Blossom where the rose should grow;
I shall sing when night's decay
Ushers in a drearier day.

EMILY BRONTË

23 **To Autumn**

Season of mists and mellow fruitfulness,
  Close bosom-friend of the maturing sun;
Conspiring with him how to load and bless
  With fruit the vines that round the thatch-eaves run;
To bend with apples the mossed cottage-trees,
  And fill all fruit with ripeness to the core;

To swell the gourd, and plump the hazel shells
With a sweet kernel; to set budding more,
And still more, later flowers for the bees,
Until they think warm days will never cease;
For Summer has o'erbrimmed their clammy cells.

Who hath not seen thee oft amid thy store?
Sometimes whoever seeks abroad may find
Thee sitting careless on a granary floor,
Thy hair soft-lifted by the winnowing wind;
Or on a half-reaped furrow sound asleep,
Drowsed with the fume of poppies, while thy hook
Spares the next swath and all its twinèd flowers;
And sometimes like a gleaner thou dost keep
Steady thy laden head across a brook;
Or by a cider-press, with patient look,
Thou watchest the last oozings, hours by hours.

Where are the songs of Spring? Ay, where are they?
Think not of them, thou hast thy music too, –
While barrèd clouds bloom the soft-dying day
And touch the stubble-plains with rosy hue;
Then in a wailful choir the small gnats mourn
Among the river sallows, borne aloft
Or sinking as the light wind lives or dies;
And full-grown lambs loud bleat from hilly bourn;
Hedge-crickets sing; and now with treble soft
The red-breast whistles from a garden-croft,
And gathering swallows twitter in the skies.

JOHN KEATS

24 **Ode to the West Wind**

1

O wild West Wind, thou breath of Autumn's being,
Thou, from whose unseen presence the leaves dead
Are driven, like ghosts from an enchanter fleeing,

Yellow, and black, and pale, and hectic red,
Pestilence-stricken multitudes! O thou
Who chariotest to their dark wintry bed

The wingèd seeds, where they lie cold and low,
Each like a corpse within its grave, until
Thine azure sister of the Spring shall blow

Her clarion o'er the dreaming earth, and fill
(Driving sweet buds like flocks to feed in air)
With living hues and odours plain and hill:

Wild Spirit, which art moving everywhere;
Destroyer and Preserver; hear, O, hear!

2

Thou on whose stream, 'mid the steep sky's commotion
Loose clouds like earth's decaying leaves are shed,
Shook from the tangled boughs of heaven and ocean,

Angels of rain and lightning! there are spread
On the blue surface of thine airy surge,
Like the bright hair uplifted from the head

Of some fierce Maenad, even from the dim verge
  Of the horizon to the zenith's height,
The locks of the approaching storm. Thou dirge

Of the dying year, to which this closing night
  Will be the dome of a vast sepulchre,
Vaulted with all thy congregated might

Of vapours, from whose solid atmosphere
Black rain, and fire, and hail, will burst: O, hear!

3

Thou who didst waken from his summer dreams
  The blue Mediterranean, where he lay,
Lulled by the coil of his crystalline streams,

Beside a pumice isle in Baiae's bay,
  And saw in sleep old palaces and towers
Quivering within the wave's intenser day,

All overgrown with azure moss, and flowers
  So sweet, the sense faints picturing them! Thou
For whose path the Atlantic's level powers

Cleave themselves into chasms, while far below
  The sea-blooms and the oozy woods which wear
The sapless foliage of the ocean, know

Thy voice, and suddenly grow gray with fear,
And tremble and despoil themselves: O, hear!

4

If I were a dead leaf thou mightest bear;
  If I were a swift cloud to fly with thee;
A wave to pant beneath thy power, and share

The impulse of thy strength, only less free
  Than thou, O uncontrollable! If even
I were as in my boyhood, and could be

The comrade of thy wanderings over heaven,
  As then, when to outstrip thy skiey speed
Scarce seemed a vision, I would ne'er have striven

As thus with thee in prayer in my sore need.
  O! lift me as a wave, a leaf, a cloud!
I fall upon the thorns of life! I bleed!

A heavy weight of hours has chained and bowed
One too like thee – tameless, and swift, and proud.

5

Make me thy lyre, even as the forest is:
  What if my leaves are falling like its own!
The tumult of thy mighty harmonies

Will take from both a deep autumnal tone,
  Sweet though in sadness. Be thou, Spirit fierce,
My spirit! Be thou me, impetuous one!

Drive my dead thoughts over the universe,
  Like withered leaves to quicken a new birth;
And, by the incantation of this verse,

Scatter, as from an unextinguished hearth
  Ashes and sparks, my words among mankind!
Be through my lips to unawakened earth

The trumpet of a prophecy! O Wind,
If Winter comes, can Spring be far behind?

PERCY BYSSHE SHELLEY

25 North Wind in October

In the golden glade the chestnuts are fallen all;
From the sered boughs of the oak the acorns fall:
The beech scatters her ruddy fire;
The lime hath stripped to the cold,
And standeth naked above her yellow attire:
The larch thinneth her spire
To lay the ways of the wood with cloth of gold.

  Out of the golden-green and white
Of the brake the fir-trees stand upright
In the forest of flame, and wave aloft
To the blue of heaven their blue-green tuftings soft.

But swiftly in shuddering gloom the splendours fail,
As the harrying North-wind beareth
A cloud of skirmishing hail
The grievèd woodland to smite:
In a hurricane through the trees he teareth,
Raking the boughs and the leaves rending,
And whistleth to the descending
Blows of his icy flail.

Gold and snow he mixeth in spite,
And whirleth afar; as away on his winnowing flight
He passeth, and all again for awhile is bright.

ROBERT BRIDGES

26 Wind

This house has been far out at sea all night,
The woods crashing through darkness, the booming
hills,
Winds stampeding the fields under the window
Floundering black astride and blinding wet

Till day rose; then under an orange sky
The hills had new places, and wind wielded
Blade-like, luminous black and emerald,
Flexing like the lens of a mad eye.

At noon I scaled along the house-side as far as
The coal-house door. I dared once to look up –
Through the brunt wind that dented the balls of my
eyes
The tent of the hills drummed and strained its guyrope,

The fields quivering, the skyline a grimace,
At any second to bang and vanish with a flap:
The wind flung a magpie away and a black-
Back gull bent like an iron bar slowly. The house

Rang like some fine green goblet in the note
That any second would shatter it. Now deep
In chairs, in front of the great fire, we grip
Our hearts and cannot entertain book, thought,

Or each other. We watch the fire blazing,
And feel the roots of the house move, but sit on,
Seeing the window tremble to come in,
Hearing the stones cry out under the horizons.

TED HUGHES

27 **Snow in the Suburbs**

Every branch big with it,
Bent every twig with it;
Every fork like a white web-foot;
Every street and pavement mute:
Some flakes have lost their way, and grope back
upward, when
Meeting those meandering down they turn and descend
again.
The palings are glued together like a wall,
And there is no waft of wind with the fleecy fall.

A sparrow enters the tree,
Whereon immediately
A snow-lump thrice his own slight size
Descends on him and showers his head and eyes.
And overturns him,
And near inurns him,
And lights on a nether twig, when its brush
Starts off a volley of other lodging lumps with a rush.

The steps are a blanched slope,
Up which, with feeble hope,
A black cat comes, wide-eyed and thin;
And we take him in.

THOMAS HARDY

28 Aubade

The snow still falls in dry and powdery grains,
Fills the green footprints on the whitened grass;
A gusty wind still turns the weather-vanes
And whirls a frosted leaf about a court
Where boys are sliding, while a pane of glass
Cracks in the cold with a subdued report.

Last night that snow more grossly, densely fell;
Each antlered tree tossed flakes upon its tines,
And whiteness filled the gaping of each cell
In an old wasps' nest hanging from a bough
That held it to the storm; those tell-tale lines
Upon the black sward were not made till now.

For it was I, who, wakened by a light
That made the close-drawn bedroom curtains glow
Too soon for the dead season, and too bright,
Felt then a chill through blankets to the bone
Which told that while I slept there had been snow,
Went down to tread it, early and alone.

EDWARD LUCIE-SMITH

29 November

The lonely season in lonely lands, when fled
Are half the birds, and mists lie low, and the sun
Is rarely seen, nor strayeth far from his bed;
The short days pass unwelcomed one by one.

   Out by the ricks the mantled engine stands
Crestfallen, deserted, – for now all hands
Are told to the plough, – and ere it is dawn appear
The teams following and crossing far and near,
As hour by hour they broaden the brown bands
Of the striped fields; and behind them firk and prance
The heavy rooks, and daws grey-pated dance:
As awhile, surmounting a crest, in sharp outline
(A miniature of toil, a gem's design,)
They are pictured, horses and men, or now near by
Above the lane they shout lifting the share,
By the trim hedgerow bloomed with purple air;
Where, under the thorns, dead leaves in huddle lie

Packed by the gales of Autumn, and in and out
The small wrens glide
With a happy note of cheer,
And yellow amorets flutter above and about,
Gay, familiar in fear.

And now, if the night shall be cold, across the sky
Linnets and twites, in small flocks helter-skelter,
All the afternoon to the gardens fly,
From thistle-pastures hurrying to gain shelter
Of American rhododendron or cherry-laurel:
And here and there, near chilly setting of sun,
In an isolated tree a congregation
Of starlings chatter and chide,
Thickset as summer leaves, in garrulous quarrel:
Suddenly they hush as one, –
The tree top springs, –
And off, with a whirr of wings,
They fly by the score
To the holly-thicket, and there with myriads more
Dispute for the roosts; and from the unseen nation
A babel of tongues, like running water unceasing,
Makes live the wood, the flocking cries increasing,
Wrangling discordantly, incessantly,
While falls the night on them self-occupied;
The long dark night, that lengthens slow,
Deepening with Winter to starve grass and tree,
And soon to bury in snow
The Earth, that, sleeping 'neath her frozen stole,
Shall dream a dream crept from the sunless pole
Of how her end shall be.

ROBERT BRIDGES

30 **Winter, the Huntsman**

Through his iron glades
Rides Winter the Huntsman,
All colour fades
As his horn is heard sighing.

Far through the forest
His wild hooves crash and thunder
Till many a mighty branch
Is torn asunder.

And the red reynard creeps
To his hole near the river,
The copper leaves fall
And the bare trees shiver.

As night creeps from the ground,
Hides each tree from its brother
And each dying sound
Reveals yet another.

Is it Winter the Huntsman
Who gallops through his iron glades,
Cracking his cruel whip
To the gathering shades?

OSBERT SITWELL

31 **Winter** (From *Love's Labour's Lost*)

When icicles hang by the wall,
  And Dick the shepherd blows his nail,
And Tom bears logs into the hall,
  And milk comes frozen home in pail,
When blood is nipped and ways be foul,
Then nightly sings the staring owl,
                    Tu-whit,
Tu-who, a merry note,
While greasy Joan doth keel the pot.

When all aloud the wind doth blow,
  And coughing drowns the parson's saw,
And birds sit brooding in the snow,
  And Marian's nose looks red and raw,
When roasted crabs hiss in the bowl,
Then nightly sings the staring owl,
                    Tu-whit,
Tu-who, a merry note,
While greasy Joan doth keel the pot.

WILLIAM SHAKESPEARE

32 **November**

The shepherds almost wonder where they dwell,
And the old dog for his right journey stares;
The path leads somewhere, but they cannot tell,
And neighbour meets with neighbour unawares.
The maiden passes close beside her cow,
And wanders on, and thinks her far away;
The ploughman goes unseen behind his plough
And seems to lose his horses half the day.

The lazy mist creeps on in journey slow;
The maidens shout and wonder where they go;
So dull and dark are the November days.
The lazy mist high up the evening curled,
And now the moon quite hides in smoke and haze;
The place we occupy seems all the world.

JOHN CLARE

33 **The Winter Trees**

Against the evening sky the trees are black,
Iron themselves against the iron rails;
The hurrying crowds seek cinemas or homes,
A cosy hour where warmth will mock the wind.
They do not look at trees now summer's gone,
For fallen with their leaves are those glad days
Of sand and sea and ships, of swallows, lambs,
Of cricket teams, and walking long in woods.

Standing among the trees, a shadow bends
And picks a cigarette-end from the ground;
It lifts the collar of an overcoat,
And blows upon its hands and stamps its feet.–
For this is winter, chastiser of the free,
This is winter, kind only to the bound.

CLIFFORD DYMENT

34 **November**

The month of the drowned dog. After the long rain
  the land
Was sodden as the bed of an ancient lake,
Treed with iron and birdless. In the sunk lane
The ditch – a seep silent all summer –

Made brown foam with a big voice: that, and my
  boots
On the lane's scrubbed stones, in the gulleyed leaves,
Against the hill's hanging silence;
Mist silvering the droplets on the bare thorns

Slower than the change of daylight.
In a let of the ditch a tramp was bundled asleep:
Face tucked down into beard, drawn in
Under its hair like a hedgehog's. I took him for dead,

But his stillness separated from the death
Of the rotting grass and the ground. A wind chilled,
And a fresh comfort tightened through him,
Each hand stuffed deeper into the other sleeve.

His ankles, bound with sacking and hairy band,
Rubbed each other, resettling. The wind hardened;
A puff shook a glittering from the thorns,
And again the rains' dragging grey columns

Smudged the farms. In a moment
The fields were jumping and smoking; the thorns
Quivered, riddled with the glassy verticals.
I stayed on under the welding cold

Watching the tramp's face glisten and the drops on his
  coat
Flash and darken. I thought what strong trust
Slept in him – as the trickling furrows slept,
And the thorn-roots in their grip on darkness;

And the buried stones, taking the weight of winter;
The hill where the hare crouched with clenched teeth.
Rain plastered the land till it was shining
Like hammered lead, and I ran, and in the rushing
  wood

Shuttered by a black oak leaned.
The keeper's gibbet had owls and hawks
By the neck, weasels, a gang of cats, crows:
Some, stiff, weightless, twirled like dry bark bits

In the drilling rain. Some still had their shape,
Had their pride with it; hung, chins on chests,
Patient to outwit these worst days that beat
Their crowns bare and dripped from their feet.

TED HUGHES

35 **Spring Song in Winter**

Too long, too long
I gathered icicles in spring
To thread them for a melting song;
And in midsummer saw the foliage fall,
Too foolish then to sing
How leaf and petal cling
Though wind would bear them to the root of all.

Now winter's come, and winter proves me wrong:
Dark in my garden the dead,
Great naked briars, have spread,
So vastly multiplied
They almost hide
The single shrub to share whose blossoming
Blood on cold thorns my fingers shed.

MICHAEL HAMBURGER

36 **Late Snow**

The heavy train through the dim country went rolling, rolling
Interminably, passing misty snow-covered ploughland ridges
That merged in the snowy sky; came turning meadows, fences,
Came gullies and passed, and ice-coloured streams under frozen bridges.

Across the travelling landscape evenly drooped and lifted
The telegraph wires, thick ropes of snow in the windless air;
They drooped and paused and lifted again to unseen summits,
Drawing the eyes and soothing them, often to a drowsy stare.

Singly in the snow the ghosts of trees were softly pencilled,
Fainter and fainter, in distance fading, into nothingness gliding,
But sometimes a crowd of the intricate silver trees of fairyland
Passed, marvellous close and clear, the phantom world hiding.

O untroubled these moving mantled miles of shadow-
less shadows,
And lovely the film of falling flakes, so wayward and
slack:
But I thought of many a mother-bird screening her
nestlings,
Sitting silent with wide bright eyes, snow on her back.

J. C. SQUIRE

37 **London Snow**

When men were all asleep the snow came flying,
In large white flakes falling on the city brown,
Stealthily and perpetually settling and loosely lying,
Hushing the latest traffic of the drowsy town;
Deadening, muffling, stifling its murmurs failing;
Lazily and incessantly floating down and down;
Silently sifting and veiling road, roof and railing;
Hiding difference, making unevenness even,
Into angles and crevices softly drifting and sailing.
All night it fell, and when full inches seven
It lay in the depth of its uncompacted lightness,
The clouds blew off from a high and frosty heaven;
And all woke earlier for the unaccustomed brightness
Of the winter dawning, the strange unheavenly glare.
The eye marvelled – marvelled at the dazzling
whiteness;
The ear hearkened to the stillness of the solemn air;

No sound of wheel rumbling nor of foot falling,
And the busy morning cries came thin and spare.
  Then boys I heard, as they went to school, calling;
They gathered up the crystal manna to freeze
Their tongues with tasting, their hands with snow-
    balling;
  Or rioted in a drift, plunging up to the knees;
Or peering up from under the white-mossed wonder,
"O look at the trees!" they cried, "O look at the
    trees!"
  With lessened load a few carts creak and blunder,
Following along the white deserted way,
A country company long dispersed asunder:
  When now already the sun, in pale display
Standing by Paul's high dome, spread forth below
His sparkling beams, and awoke the stir of the day.
  For now doors open, and war is waged with the
    snow;
And trains of sombre men, past tale of number,
Tread long brown paths, as toward their toil they go;
  But even for them awhile no cares encumber
Their minds diverted; the daily word is unspoken,
The daily thoughts of labour and sorrow slumber
At the sight of the beauty that greets them, for the
    charm they have broken.

ROBERT BRIDGES

38 The Snow

In no way that I chose to go
Could I escape the falling snow.

I shut my eyes, wet with my fears:
The snow still whispered at my ears.

I stopped my ears in deaf disguise:
The snow still fell before my eyes.

Snow was my comrade, snow my fate,
In a country huge and desolate.

My footsteps made a shallow space,
And then the snow filled up the place,

And all the walking I had done
Was on a journey not begun.

I did not know the distance gone,
But resolutely travelled on,

While silently on every hand
Fell the sorrow of the land,

And no way that I chose to go
Could lead me from the grief of snow.

CLIFFORD DYMENT

39 **Skating on the Lake** (From *The Prelude*)

And in the frosty season, when the sun
Was set, and visible for many a mile
The cottage windows blazed through twilight gloom,
I heeded not their summons. Happy time
It was indeed for all of us – for me
It was a time of rapture! Clear and loud
The village clock tolled six, I wheeled about,
Proud and exulting like an untired horse
That cares not for his home. All shod with steel,

We hissed along the polished ice in games
Confederate, imitative of the chase
And woodland pleasures, the resounding horn,
The pack loud chiming, and the hunted hare.
So through the darkness and the cold we flew,
And not a voice was idle; with the din
Smitten, the precipices rang aloud;
The leafless trees and every icy crag
Tinkled like iron; while far distant hills
Into the tumult sent an alien sound
Of melancholy not unnoticed, while the stars
Eastward were sparkling clear, and in the west
The orange sky of evening died away.
Not seldom from the uproar I retired
Into a silent bay, or sportively
Glanced sideway, leaving the tumultuous throng,
To cut across the reflex of a star
That fled, and, flying still before me, gleamed
Upon the glassy plain; and oftentimes,
When we had given our bodies to the wind,
And all the shadowy banks on either side
Came sweeping through the darkness, spinning still
The rapid line of motion, then at once
Have I, reclining back upon my heels,
Stopped short. Yet still the solitary cliffs
Wheeled by me – even as if the earth had rolled
With visible motion her diurnal round!
Behind me did they stretch in solemn train,
Feebler and feebler, and I stood and watched
Till all was tranquil as a dreamless sleep.

WILLIAM WORDSWORTH

40 **Midnight Skaters**

The hop-poles stand in cones,
  The icy pond lurks under,
The pole-tops steeple to the thrones
  Of stars, sound gulfs of wonder;
But not the tallest there, 'tis said,
Could fathom to this pond's black bed.

Then is not death at watch
  Within those secret waters?
What wants he but to catch
  Earth's heedless sons and daughters?
With but a crystal parapet
Between, he has his engines set.

Then on, blood shouts, on, on,
  Twirl, wheel and whip above him,
Dance on this ball-floor thin and wan,
  Use him as though you love him;
Court him, elude him, reel and pass,
And let him hate you through the glass.

EDMUND BLUNDEN

41 A Hard Frost

A frost came in the night and stole my world
And left this changeling for it – a precocious
Image of spring, too brilliant to be true:
White lilac on the windowpane, each grass-blade
Furred like a catkin, maydrift loading the hedge.
The elms behind the house are elms no longer
But blossomers in crystal, stems of the mist
That hangs yet in the valley below, amorphous
As the blind tissue whence creation formed.
  The sun looks out, and the fields blaze with
    diamonds.
Mockery spring, to lend this bridal gear
For a few hours to a raw country maid,
Then leave her all disconsolate with old fairings
Of aconite and snowdrop! No, not here
Amid this flounce and filigree of death
Is the real transformation scene in progress,
But deep below where frost
Worrying the stiff clods unclenches their
Grip on the seed and lets our future breathe.

C. DAY LEWIS

Poetry lifts the veil from the hidden beauty of the world, and makes familiar objects be as if they were not familiar.

Percy Bysshe Shelley

42 **Country Life** (From *As You Like It*)

Now, my co-mates and brothers in exile,
Hath not old custom made this life more sweet
Than that of painted pomp? Are not these woods
More free from peril than the envious court?
Here feel we but the penalty of Adam,
The seasons' difference; as the icy fang
And churlish chiding of the winter's wind,
Which, when it bites and blows upon my body,
Even till I shrink with cold, I smile and say,
"This is no flattery; these are counsellors
That feelingly persuade me what I am."
Sweet are the uses of adversity,
Which, like the toad, ugly and venomous,
Wears yet a precious jewel in his head;
And this our life, exempt from public haunt,
Finds tongues in trees, books in the running brooks,
Sermons in stones, and good in everything.

WILLIAM SHAKESPEARE

43 **To One Who Has Been Long in City Pent**

To one who has been long in city pent,
  'Tis very sweet to look into the fair
  And open face of heaven, – to breathe a prayer
Full in the smile of the blue firmament.
Who is more happy, when, with heart's content,
  Fatigued he sinks into some pleasant lair
  Of wavy grass, and reads a debonair
And gentle tale of love and languishment?
Returning home at evening, with an ear
  Catching the notes of Philomel, – an eye
Watching the sailing cloudlet's bright career,
  He mourns that day so soon has glided by:
E'en like the passage of an angel's tear
  That falls through the clear ether silently.

JOHN KEATS

44 Farm Scene

The cow-boy shuns the shower and seeks the mat
To clean his shoes, and swings his napless hat
And drags his faggot in, a glad supply,
While laughing maidens help his clothes to dry.
The butter is made up, the bever set,
And all the ploughmen in the kitchen met;
One runs about the new-laid eggs to find,
One gets the garden beans with flannel lined
And pelts the laughing maidens with the shells;
And in the brier bush where the robin dwells
The tender maiden runs and carries crumbs;
Close to the door the fighting sparrow comes;
A maiden runs and shakes the damsons down
And hides them in her apron for the clown;
One takes a handful first and runs away,
And so they keep half work, half holiday.

JOHN CLARE

45 The Shepherd

How sweet is the shepherd's sweet lot.
    From the morn to the evening he strays;
He shall follow his sheep all the day,
    And his tongue shall be fillèd with praise.

For he hears the lambs' innocent call,
    And he hears the ewes' tender reply;
He is watchful while they are in peace,
    For they know when their shepherd is nigh.

WILLIAM BLAKE

46 A Peasant

Iago Prytherch his name, though, be it allowed,
Just an ordinary man of the bald Welsh hills,
Who pens a few sheep in a gap of cloud.
Docking mangels, chipping the green skin
From the yellow bones with a half-witted grin
Of satisfaction, or churning the crude earth
To a stiff sea of clods that glint in the wind –
So are his days spent, his spittled mirth
Rarer than the sun that cracks the cheeks
Of the gaunt sky perhaps once in a week.
And then at night see him fixed in his chair
Motionless, except when he leans to gob in the fire.
There is something frightening in the vacancy of his
  mind.
His clothes, sour with years of sweat
And animal contact, shock the refined,
But affected, sense with their stark naturalness.
Yet this is your prototype, who, season by season
Against siege of rain and the wind's attrition,
Preserves his stock, an impregnable fortress
Not to be stormed even in death's confusion.
Remember him then, for he, too, is a winner of wars,
Enduring like a tree under the curious stars.

R. S. THOMAS

47 A Boy's Song

Where the pools are bright and deep,
Where the gray trout lies asleep,
Up the river and over the lea,
That's the way for Billy and me.

Where the blackbird sings the latest,
Where the hawthorn blooms the sweetest,
Where the nestlings chirp and flee,
That's the way for Billy and me.

Where the mowers mow the cleanest,
Where the hay lies thick and greenest,
There to track the homeward bee,
That's the way for Billy and me.

Where the hazel bank is steepest,
Where the shadow falls the deepest,
Where the clustering nuts fall free,
That's the way for Billy and me.

Why the boys should drive away
Little sweet maidens from their play,
Or love to banter and fight so well,
That's the thing I never could tell.

But this I know, I love to play
Through the meadow, among the hay,
Up the water and over the lea,
That's the way for Billy and me.

JAMES HOGG

48 Sowing

It was a perfect day
For sowing; just
As sweet and dry was the ground
As tobacco-dust.

I tasted deep the hour
Between the far
Owl's chuckling first soft cry
And the first star.

A long stretched hour it was;
Nothing undone
Remained; the early seeds
All safely sown.

And now, hark at the rain,
Windless and light,
Half a kiss, half a tear,
Saying good-night.

EDWARD THOMAS

49 The Solitary Reaper

Behold her, single in the field,
  Yon solitary Highland Lass!
Reaping and singing by herself;
  Stop here, or gently pass!
Alone she cuts and binds the grain,
And sings a melancholy strain;
O listen! for the Vale profound
Is overflowing with the sound.

No Nightingale did ever chaunt
  More welcome notes to weary bands
Of travellers in some shady haunt,
  Among Arabian sands:
A voice so thrilling ne'er was heard
In spring-time from the Cuckoo-bird,
Breaking the silence of the seas
Among the farthest Hebrides.

Will no one tell me what she sings?
  Perhaps the plaintive numbers flow
For old, unhappy, far-off things,
  And battles long ago:
Or is it some more humble lay,
  Familiar matter of to-day?
Some natural sorrow, loss, or pain,
  That has been, and may be again?

Whate'er the theme, the Maiden sang
  As if her song could have no ending;
I saw her singing at her work,
  And o'er the sickle bending;
I listened, motionless and still;
And, as I mounted up the hill,
The music in my heart I bore,
Long after it was heard no more.

WILLIAM WORDSWORTH

50 Cambridgeshire

The stacks, like blunt impassive temples, rise
Across flat fields against autumnal skies.
The hairy-hoovèd horses plough the land,
Or as in prayer and meditation stand
Upholding square, primeval, dung-stained carts,
With an unending patience in their hearts.

Nothing is changed. The farmer's gig goes by
Against the horizon. Surely the same sky,
So vast and yet familiar, grey and mild,
And streaked with light like music, I, a child,
Lifted my face from leaf-edged lanes to see,
Late-coming home, to bread-and-butter tea.

FRANCES CORNFORD

51 **Mending Wall**

Something there is that doesn't love a wall,
That sends the frozen-ground-swell under it,
And spills the upper boulders in the sun;
And makes gaps even two can pass abreast.
The work of hunters is another thing:
I have come after them and made repair
Where they have left not one stone on a stone,
But they would have the rabbit out of hiding,
To please the yelping dogs. The gaps I mean,
No one has seen them made or heard them made,
But at spring mending-time we find them there.
I let my neighbour know beyond the hill;
And on a day we meet to walk the line
And set the wall between us once again.
We keep the wall between us as we go.
To each the boulders that have fallen to each.
And some are loaves and some so nearly balls
We have to use a spell to make them balance:
"Stay where you are until our backs are turned!"
We wear our fingers rough with handling them.
Oh, just another kind of outdoor game,
One on a side. It comes to little more:
There where it is we do not need the wall:
He is all pine and I am apple orchard.
My apple trees will never get across
And eat the cones under his pines, I tell him.
He only says, "Good fences make good neighbours."
Spring is the mischief in me, and I wonder
If I could put a notion in his head:
"*Why* do they make good neighbours? Isn't it

Where there are cows? But here there are no cows.
Before I built a wall I'd ask to know
What I was walling in or walling out,
And to whom I was like to give offence.
Something there is that doesn't love a wall,
That wants it down." I could say "Elves" to him,
But it's not elves exactly, and I'd rather
He said it for himself. I see him there
Bringing a stone grasped firmly by the top
In each hand, like an old-stone savage armed.
He moves in darkness as it seems to me,
Not of woods only and the shade of trees.
He will not go behind his father's saying,
And he likes having thought of it so well
He says again, "Good fences make good neighbours."

ROBERT FROST

52 The Mill-Pond

The sun blazed while the thunder yet
Added a boom:
A wagtail flickered bright over
The mill-pond's gloom:

Less than the cooing in the alder
Isles of the pool
Sounded the thunder through that plunge
Of waters cool.

Scared starlings on the aspen tip
Past the black mill
Outchattered the stream and the next roar
Far on the hill.

As my feet dangling teased the foam
That slid below
A girl came out. "Take care!" she said –
Ages ago.

She startled me, standing quite close
Dressed all in white:
Ages ago I was angry till
She passed from sight.

Then the storm burst, and as I crouched
To shelter, how
Beautiful and kind, too, she seemed,
As she does now!

EDWARD THOMAS

53 Flame and Snow

The bare branches rose against the grey sky.
Under them, freshly fallen, snow shone to the eye.

Up the hill-slope, over the brow it shone,
Spreading an immaterial beauty to tread upon.

In the elbow of black boughs it clung, nested white,
And smooth below it slept in the solitude of its light.

It was deep to the knee in the hollow; there in a stump
  of wood
I stuck my bill-hook, warm to the finger's blood, and
  stood,

Pausing, and breathed and listened: all the air around
Was filled with busy strokes and ringing of clean
   sound,

And now and again a crack and a slow rending, to tell
When a tree heavily tottered and swift with a crash
   fell.

I smelt the woody smell of smoke from the fire, now
Beginning to spurt from frayed bracken and torn
   bough

In the lee of a drift, fed from our long morning toil
And sending smart to the eyes the smoke in a blue coil.

I lopped the twigs from a fresh-cut pole and tossed it
   aside
To the stakes heaped beyond me, and made a plunging
   stride,

And gathered twines of bramble and dead hazel sticks
And a faggot of twisted thorn with snow lumped in
   the pricks,

And piled the smoulder high. Soon a blaze tore
Up through hissing boughs and shrivelling leaves,
   from a core

Of quivering crimson; soon the heat burst and revelled,
And apparitions of little airy flames dishevelled

Gleamed and vanished, a lost flight of elfin wings,
Trembling aloft to the wild music that Fire sings

Dancing alive from nothing, lovely and mad. And
still
The snow, pale as a dream, slept on the old hill,

Softly fallen and strange. Which made me more to
glow,
Beauty of young flames, or wonder of young snow?

LAURENCE BINYON

54 Throwing a Tree: New Forest

The two executioners stalk along over the knolls,
Bearing two axes with heavy heads shining and wide,
And a long limp two-handled saw toothed for
cutting great boles,
And so they approach the proud tree that bears the
death-mark on its side.

Jackets doffed they swing axes and chop away just
above ground,
And the chips fly about and lie white on the moss
and fallen leaves;
Till a broad deep gash in the bark is hewn all the
way round,
And one of them tries to hook upward a rope, which
at last he achieves.

The saw then begins, till the top of the tall giant
shivers:
The shivers are seen to grow greater each cut than
before:

They edge out the saw, tug the rope: but the tree only quivers,
And kneeling and sawing again, they step back to try pulling once more.

Then, lastly, the living mast sways, further sways: with a shout
Job and Ike rush aside. Reached the end of its long staying powers
The tree crashes downward: it shakes all its neighbours throughout,
And two hundred years' steady growth has been ended in less than two hours.

THOMAS HARDY

55 The Line-Gang

Here come the line-gang pioneering by.
They throw a forest down less cut than broken.
They plant dead trees for living, and the dead
They string together with a living thread.
They string an instrument against the sky
Wherein words, whether beaten out or spoken,
Will run as hushed as when they were a thought.
But in no hush they string it: they go past
With shouts afar to pull the cable taut,
To hold it hard until they make it fast,
To ease away – they have it. With a laugh
And oath of towns that set the wild at naught,
They bring the telephone and the telegraph.

ROBERT FROST

56 The Pylons

The secret of these hills was stone, and cottages
Of that stone made,
And crumbling roads
That turned on sudden hidden villages.

Now over these small hills they have built the concrete
That trails black wire;
Pylons, those pillars
Bare like nude, giant girls that have no secret.

The valley with its gilt and evening look
And the green chestnut
Of customary root
Are mocked dry like the parched bed of a brook.

But far above and far as sight endures
Like whips of anger
With lightning's danger
There runs the quick perspective of the future.

This dwarfs our emerald country by its trek
So tall with prophecy:
Dreaming of cities
Where often clouds shall lean their swan-white neck.

STEPHEN SPENDER

57 Tall Nettles

Tall nettles cover up, as they have done
These many springs, the rusty harrow, the plough
Long worn out, and the roller made of stone:
Only the elm butt tops the nettles now.

This corner of the farmyard I like most:
As well as any bloom upon a flower
I like the dust on the nettles, never lost
Except to prove the sweetness of a shower.

EDWARD THOMAS

58 Good-Bye and Keep Cold

This saying good-bye on the edge of the dark
And the cold to an orchard so young in the bark
Reminds me of all that can happen to harm
An orchard away at the end of the farm
All winter, cut off by a hill from the house.
I don't want it girdled by rabbit and mouse,
I don't want it dreamily nibbled for browse
By deer, and I don't want it budded by grouse.
(If certain it wouldn't be idle to call
I'd summon grouse, rabbit, and deer to the wall
And warn them away with a stick for a gun.)
I don't want it stirred by the heat of the sun.
(We made it secure against being, I hope,
By setting it out on a northerly slope.)
No orchard's the worse for the wintriest storm;
But one thing about it, it mustn't get warm.
"How often already you've had to be told,
Keep cold, young orchard. Good-bye and keep cold.
Dread fifty above more than fifty below."
I have to be gone for a season or so.
My business awhile is with different trees,
Less carefully nurtured, less fruitful than these,
And such as is done to their wood with an axe –
Maples and birches and tamaracks.
I wish I could promise to lie in the night
And think of an orchard's arboreal plight
When slowly (and nobody comes with a light)
Its heart sinks lower under the sod.
But something has to be left to God.

ROBERT FROST

59 The Evening Comes

The evening comes, the fields are still.
The tinkle of the thirsty rill,
Unheard all day, ascends again;
Deserted is the half-mown plain,
Silent the sheaves, the ringing wain,
The reaper's cry, the dog's alarms,
All housed within the sleeping farms!
The business of the day is done,
The last belated gleaner gone.
And from the thyme upon the height,
And from the elder blossom white,
And pale dog-roses in the hedge,
And from the mint plant in the sedge,
In puffs of balm the night air blows
The perfume which the day forgoes.
And on the pure horizon far,
See pulsing with the first-born star,
The liquid sky above the hill!
The evening comes, the field is still.

MATTHEW ARNOLD

To be a poet is to apprehend the true and the beautiful.

Percy Bysshe Shelley

60 A Fine Day

Clear had the day been from the dawn,
   All chequered was the sky,
Thin clouds like scarfs of cobweb lawn
   Veiled heaven's most glorious eye.
The wind had no more strength than this,
   That leisurely it blew,
To make one leaf the next to kiss
   That closely by it grew.

MICHAEL DRAYTON

61 I Stood Tip-Toe upon a Little Hill

I stood tip-toe upon a little hill,
The air was cooling, and so very still,
That the sweet buds which with a modest pride
Pull droopingly, in slanting curve aside,
Their scantly leaved, and finely tapering stems,
Had not yet lost those starry diadems
Caught from the early sobbing of the morn.
The clouds were pure and white as flocks new shorn,
And fresh from the clear brook; sweetly they slept
On the blue fields of heaven, and then there crept
A little noiseless noise among the leaves,
Born of the very sigh that silence heaves;
For not the faintest motion could be seen
Of all the shades that slanted o'er the green.
There was wide wand'ring for the greediest eye,
To peer about upon variety;
Far round the horizon's crystal air to skim,
And trace the dwindled edgings of its brim;
To picture out the quaint and curious bending
Of a fresh woodland alley, never ending;
Or by the bowery clefts, and leafy shelves,
Guess where the jaunty streams refresh themselves.
I gazed awhile, and felt as light and free
As though the fanning wings of Mercury
Had played upon my heels: I was light-hearted.
And many pleasures to my vision started;
So I straightway began to pluck a posy
Of luxuries bright, milky, soft and rosy.

JOHN KEATS

62 The Cloud

I bring fresh showers for the thirsting flowers,
  From the seas and the streams;
I bear light shade for the leaves when laid
  In their noonday dreams.
From my wings are shaken the dews that waken
  The sweet buds every one,
When rocked to rest on their mother's breast,
  As she dances about the sun.
I wield the flail of the lashing hail,
  And whiten the green plains under,
And then again I dissolve it in rain,
  And laugh as I pass in thunder.

I sift the snow on the mountains below,
  And their great pines groan aghast;
And all the night 'tis my pillow white,
  While I sleep in the arms of the blast.
Sublime on the towers of my skiey bowers,
  Lightning my pilot sits;
In a cavern under is fettered the thunder,
  It struggles and howls at fits;
Over earth and ocean, with gentle motion,
  This pilot is guiding me,
Lured by the love of the genii that move
  In the depths of the purple sea;
Over the rills, and the crags, and the hills,
  Over the lakes and the plains,
Wherever he dream, under mountain or stream,
  The Spirit he loves remains;
And I all the while bask in Heaven's blue smile,
  Whilst he is dissolving in rains.

The sanguine Sunrise, with his meteor eyes,
  And his burning plumes outspread,
Leaps on the back of my sailing rack,
  When the morning star shines dead;
As on the jag of a mountain crag,
  Which an earthquake rocks and swings,
An eagle alit one moment may sit
  In the light of its golden wings.
And when Sunset may breathe, from the lit sea beneath,
  Its ardours of rest and of love,
And the crimson pall of eve may fall
  From the depth of Heaven above,
With wings folded I rest, on mine aëry nest,
  As still as a brooding dove.

That orbèd maiden with white fire laden,
  Whom mortals call the Moon,
Glides glimmering o'er my fleece-like floor,
  By the midnight breezes strewn;
And wherever the beat of her unseen feet,
  Which only the angels hear,
May have broken the woof of my tent's thin roof,
  The stars peep behind her and peer;
And I laugh to see them whirl and flee
  Like a swarm of golden bees,
When I widen the rent in my wind-built tent,
  Till the calm rivers, lakes, and seas,
Like strips of the sky fallen through me on high,
  Are each paved with the moon and these.

I bind the Sun's throne with a burning zone,
  And the Moon's with a girdle of pearl;
The volcanoes are dim, and the stars reel and swim,
  When the whirlwinds my banner unfurl.
From cape to cape, with a bridge-like shape,
  Over a torrent sea,
Sunbeam-proof, I hang like a roof, –
  The mountains its columns be.
The triumphal arch through which I march
  With hurricane, fire, and snow,
When the Powers of the air are chained to my chair,
  Is the million-coloured bow;
The sphere-fire above its soft colours wove,
  While the moist Earth was laughing below.

I am the daughter of Earth and Water,
  And the nursling of the Sky;
I pass through the pores of the ocean and shores;
  I change, but I cannot die.
For after the rain when with never a stain
  The pavilion of Heaven is bare,
And the winds and sunbeams with their convex gleams
  Build up the blue dome of air,
I silently laugh at my own cenotaph;
  And out of the caverns of rain,
Like a child from the womb, like a ghost from the
    tomb,
  I arise and unbuild it again.

PERCY BYSSHE SHELLEY

63 From My Diary, July 1914

Leaves
  Murmuring by myriads in the shimmering trees.
Lives
  Wakening with wonder in the Pyrenees.
Birds
  Cheerily chirping in the early day.
Bards
  Singing of summer scything through the hay.
Bees
  Shaking the heavy dews from bloom and frond.
Boys
  Bursting the surface of the ebony pond.
Flashes
  Of swimmers carving through the sparkling cold.
Fleshes
  Gleaming with wetness to the morning gold.
A mead
  Bordered about with warbling water brooks.
A maid
  Laughing the love-laugh with me; proud of looks.
The heat
  Throbbing between the upland and the peak.
Her heart
  Quivering with passion to my pressed cheek.
Braiding
  Of floating flames across the mountain brow.

Brooding
  Of stillness; and a sighing of the bough.
Stirs
  Of leaflets in the gloom; soft petal-showers;
Stars
  Expanding with the starred nocturnal flowers.

WILFRED OWEN

64 **Weathers**

This is the weather the cuckoo likes,
  And so do I;
When showers betumble the chestnut spikes,
  And nestlings fly;
And the little brown nightingale bills his best,
And they sit outside at "The Travellers' Rest",
And maids come forth sprig-muslin drest,
And citizens dream of the south and west,
  And so do I.

This is the weather the shepherd shuns,
  And so do I;
When beeches drip in browns and duns,
  And thresh, and ply;
And hill-hid tides throb, throe on throe,
And meadow rivulets overflow,
And drops in gate-bars hang in a row,
And rooks in families homeward go,
  And so do I.

THOMAS HARDY

65 **Moods of Rain**

It can be so tedious, a bore
Telling a long dull story you have heard before
So often it is meaningless;
Yet, in another mood,
It comes swashbuckling, swishing a million foils,
Feinting at daffodils, peppering tin pails,
Pelting so fast on roof, umbrella, hood,
You hear long silk being torn;
Refurbishes old toys and oils
Slick surfaces that gleam as if unworn.
Sometimes a cordial summer rain will fall
And string on railings delicate small bells;
Soundless as seeds on soil
Make green ghosts rise.
And it can be fierce, hissing like blazing thorns,
Or side-drums hammering at night-filled eyes
Until you wake and hear a long grief boil
And, overflowing, sluice
The lost raft of the world.
Yet it can come as lenitive and calm
As comfort from the mother of us all
Sighing you into sleep
Where peace prevails and only soft rains fall.

VERNON SCANNELL

66 Loveliest of Trees

Loveliest of trees, the cherry now
Is hung with bloom along the bough,
And stands about the woodland ride
Wearing white for Eastertide.

Now, of my threescore years and ten,
Twenty will not come again,
And take from seventy springs a score,
It only leaves me fifty more.

And since to look on things in bloom
Fifty springs are little room,
About the woodlands I will go
To see the cherry hung with snow.

A. E. HOUSMAN

67 **Pied Beauty**

Glory be to God for dappled things –
  For skies of couple-colour as a brinded cow;
    For rose-moles all in stipple upon trout that swim;
Fresh-firecoal chestnut-falls; finches' wings;
  Landscape plotted and pieced – fold, fallow, and
      plough;
    And all trades, their gear and tackle and trim.

All things counter, original, spare, strange;
  Whatever is fickle, freckled (who knows how?)
    With swift, slow; sweet, sour; adazzle, dim;
He fathers-forth whose beauty is past change;
    Praise him.

GERARD MANLEY HOPKINS

68 **Flying Crooked**

The butterfly, a cabbage-white,
(His honest idiocy of flight)
Will never now, it is too late,
Master the art of flying straight,
Yet has – who knows so well as I? –
A just sense of how not to fly:
He lurches here and here by guess
And God and hope and hopelessness.
Even the aerobatic swift
Has not his flying-crooked gift.

ROBERT GRAVES

69 Pleasant Sounds

The rustling of leaves under the feet in woods and
  under hedges;
The crumping of cat-ice and snow down woodrides,
  narrow lanes and every street causeway;
Rustling through a wood or rather rushing, while the
  wind halloos in the oak-top like thunder;
The rustle of birds' wings startled from their nests or
  flying unseen into the bushes;
The whizzing of larger birds overhead in a wood, such
  as crows, paddocks, buzzards;
The trample of robins and woodlarks on the brown
  leaves, and the patter of squirrels on the green moss;
The fall of an acorn on the ground, the pattering of
  nuts on the hazel branches as they fall from ripeness;
The flirt of the ground-lark's wing from the stubbles –
  how sweet such pictures on dewy mornings, when
  the dew flashes from its brown feathers!

JOHN CLARE

70 **Trees**

Of all the trees in England,
  Her sweet three corners in,
Only the Ash, the bonnie Ash
  Burns fierce while it is green.

Of all the trees in England,
  From sea to sea again,
The Willow loveliest stoops her boughs
  Beneath the driving rain.

Of all the trees in England,
  Past frankincense and myrrh,
There's none smell, of bloom and smoke,
  Like Lime and Juniper.

Of all the trees in England,
  Oak, Elder, Elm and Thorn,
The Yew alone burns lamps of peace
  For them that lie forlorn.

WALTER DE LA MARE

71 **The Brook**

I come from haunts of coot and hern,
  I make a sudden sally,
And sparkle out among the fern,
  To bicker down a valley.

By thirty hills I hurry down,
  Or slip between the ridges,
By twenty thorps, a little town,
  And half a hundred bridges.

Till last by Philip's farm I flow
  To join the brimming river,
For men may come and men may go,
  But I go on for ever.

I chatter over stony ways,
  In little sharps and trebles,
I bubble into eddying bays,
  I babble on the pebbles.

With many a curve my banks I fret
  By many a field and fallow,
And many a fairy foreland set
  With willow-weed and mallow.

I chatter, chatter, as I flow
  To join the brimming river,
For men may come and men may go,
  But I go on for ever.

I wind about, and in and out,
  With here a blossom sailing

And here and there a lusty trout,
  And here and there a grayling.

And here and there a foamy flake
  Upon me, as I travel
With many a silvery waterbreak
  Above the golden gravel,

And draw them all along, and flow
  To join the brimming river,
For men may come and men may go,
  But I go on for ever.

I steal by lawns and grassy plots,
  I slide by hazel covers;
I move the sweet forget-me-nots
  That grow for happy lovers.

I slip, I slide, I gloom, I glance,
  Among my skimming swallows;
I make the netted sunbeam dance
  Against my sandy shallows.

I murmur under moon and stars
  In brambly wildernesses;
I linger by my shingly bars;
  I loiter round my cresses;

And out again I curve and flow
  To join the brimming river,
For men may come and men may go,
  But I go on for ever.

ALFRED TENNYSON

72 The Way through the Woods

They shut the road through the woods
  Seventy years ago.
Weather and rain have undone it again,
  And now you would never know
There was once a road through the woods
  Before they planted the trees:
It is underneath the coppice and heath,
  And the thin anemones.
  Only the keeper sees
That, where the ring-dove broods
  And badgers roll at ease,
There was once a road through the woods.

Yet, if you enter the woods
  Of a summer evening late,
When the night-air cools on the trout-ringed pools
  Where the otter whistles his mate
(They fear not men in the woods
  Because they see so few),
You will hear the beat of a horse's feet
  And the swish of a skirt in the dew,
  Steadily cantering through
The misty solitudes,
  As though they perfectly knew
The old lost road through the woods . . .
But there is no road through the woods.

RUDYARD KIPLING

73 **Mushrooms**

Overnight, very
Whitely, discreetly,
Very quietly

Our toes, our noses
Take hold on the loam
Acquire the air.

Nobody sees us,
Stops us, betrays us;
The small grains make room.

Soft fists insist on
Heaving the needles,
The leafy bedding,

Even the paving,
Our hammers, our rams,
Earless and eyeless,

Perfectly voiceless,
Widen the crannies,
Shoulder through holes. We

Diet on water,
On crumbs of shadow,
Bland-mannered, asking

Little or nothing.
So many of us!
So many of us!

We are shelves, we are
Tables, we are meek,
We are edible,

Nudgers and shovers
In spite of ourselves.
Our kind multiplies:

We shall by morning
Inherit the earth.
Our foot's in the door.

SYLVIA PLATH

74 To the Evening Star

Thou fair-haired angel of the evening,
Now, whilst the sun rests on the mountains, light
Thy bright torch of love; thy radiant crown
Put on, and smile upon our evening bed.
Smile on our loves, and, while thou drawest the
Blue curtains of the sky, scatter the silver dew
On every flower that shuts its sweet eyes
In timely sleep. Let thy west wind sleep on
The lake; speak silence with thy glimmering eyes,
And wash the dusk with silver. Soon, full soon,
Dost thou withdraw; then the wolf rages wide,
And the lion glares through the dun forest:
The fleeces of our flocks are covered with
Thy sacred dew: protect them with thine influence.

WILLIAM BLAKE

75 The Evening Primrose

When once the sun sinks in the west,
And dew-drops pearl the evening's breast;
Almost as pale as moonbeams are,
Or its companionable star,
The evening primrose opes anew
Its delicate blossoms to the dew;
And, shunning hermit of the light,
Wastes its fair bloom upon the night;
Who, blindfold to its caresses,
Knows not the beauty he possesses.
Thus it blooms on till night is by
And day looks out with open eye,
Abashed at the gaze it cannot shun,
It faints and withers, and is done.

EMILY BRONTË

76 Silver

Slowly, silently, now the moon
Walks the night in her silver shoon;
This way, and that, she peers, and sees
Silver fruit upon silver trees;
One by one the casements catch
Her beams beneath the silvery thatch;
Couched in his kennel, like a log,
With paws of silver sleeps the dog;
From their shadowy cote the white breasts peep
Of doves in a silver-feathered sleep;

A harvest-mouse goes scampering by,
With silver claws, and silver eye;
And moveless fish in the water gleam,
By silver reeds in a silver stream.

WALTER DE LA MARE

77 Stars in the Moonlight

(From *The Merchant of Venice*)

How sweet the moonlight sleeps upon this bank!
Here will we sit, and let the sounds of music
Creep in our ears; soft stillness and the night
Become the touches of sweet harmony.
Sit, Jessica. Look, how the floor of heaven
Is thick inlaid with patines of bright gold.
There's not the smallest orb which thou behold'st
But in his motion like an angel sings,
Still quiring to the young-eyed cherubins.
Such harmony is in immortal souls,
But whilst this muddy vesture of decay
Doth grossly close it in, we cannot hear it.

WILLIAM SHAKESPEARE

[illegible] peeping up
Its silver [illegible]
And [illegible]
By [illegible] to a silver [illegible]

[illegible]

Stars in the Moonlight

5 ANIMALS

It is essential to poetry . . . that it be impassioned, and be able to move our feelings and awaken our affections.

Samuel Taylor Coleridge

78 The Animals

They do not live in the world,
Are not in time and space.
From birth to death hurled
No word do they have, not one
To plant a foot upon,
Were never in any place.

For with name the world was called
Out of the empty air,
With names was built and walled,
Line and circle and square,
Dust and emerald;
Snatched from deceiving death
By the articulate breath.

But these have never trod
Twice the familiar track,
Never never turned back
Into the memoried day.
All is new and near
In the unchanging Here
Of the fifth great day of God,
That shall remain the same,
Never shall pass away.

On the sixth day we came.

EDWIN MUIR

79 The Animals

I think I could turn and live with the animals, they are
so placid and self-contained;
I stand and look at them long and long.
They do not swear and whine about their condition;
They do not lie awake in the dark and weep for their
sins;
They do not make me sick discussing their duty to God;
Not one is dissatisfied – not one is demented with the
mania of owning things;
Not one kneels to another, nor to his own kind that
lived thousands of years ago;
Not one is respectable or industrious over the whole
earth.

WALT WHITMAN

80 The Bells of Heaven

'Twould ring the bells of Heaven
The wildest peal for years,
If Parson lost his senses
And people came to theirs,
And he and they together
Knelt down with angry prayers
For tamed and shabby tigers,
And dancing dogs and bears,
And wretched, blind pit-ponies,
And little hunted hares.

RALPH HODGSON

81 The Oxen

Christmas Eve, and twelve of the clock,
"Now they are all on their knees,"
An elder said as we sat in a flock
By the embers in hearthside ease.

We pictured the meek mild creatures where
They dwelt in their strawy pen,
Nor did it occur to one of us there
To doubt they were kneeling then.

So fair a fancy few would weave
In these years! Yet, I feel,
If someone said on Christmas Eve,
"Come; see the oxen kneel

"In the lonely barton by yonder coomb
Our childhood used to know,"
I should go with him in the gloom,
Hoping it might be so.

THOMAS HARDY

82 **Sheepdog Trials in Hyde Park**

For Robert Frost

A shepherd stands at one end of the arena.
Five sheep are unpenned at the other. His dog runs out
In a curve to behind them, fetches them straight to the shepherd,
Then drives the flock round a triangular course
Through a couple of gates and back to his master; two
Must be sorted there from the flock, and then all five penned.
Gathering, driving away, shedding and penning
Are the plain words for a miraculous game.

An abstract game. What can the sheepdog make of
 such
Simplified terrain? – no hills, dales, bogs, walls, tracks,
Only a quarter-mile plain of grass, dumb crowds
Like crowds on hoardings around it, and behind them
Traffic or mounds of lovers and children playing.
Well, the dog is no landscape-fancier; his whole
 concern
Is with his master's whistle, and of course
With the flock – sheep are sheep anywhere for him.

The sheep are the chanciest element. Why, for
 instance,
Go through this gate when there's on either side of it
No wall or hedge but huge and viable space?
Why not eat the grass instead of being pushed around
 it?
Like blobs of quicksilver on a tilting board
The flock erratically runs, dithers, breaks up,
Is reassembled: their ruling idea is the dog;
And behind the dog, though they know it not yet, is
 a shepherd.

The shepherd knows that time is of the essence
But haste calamitous. Between dog and sheep
There is always an ideal distance, a perfect angle;
But these are constantly varying, so the man
Should anticipate each move through the dog, his
 medium.
The shepherd is the brain behind the dog's brain,
But his control of dog, like dog's of sheep,
Is never absolute – that's the beauty of it.

For beautiful it is. The guided missiles,
The black-and-white angels follow each quirk and jink of
The evasive sheep, play grandmother's steps behind them,
Freeze to the ground, or leap to head off a straggler
Almost before it knows that it wants to stray,
As if radar-controlled. But they are not machines –
You can feel them feeling mastery, doubt, chagrin:
Machines don't frolic when their job is done.

What's needfully done in the solitude of sheep-runs –
Those tough real tasks – becomes this stylized game,
A demonstration of intuitive wit
Kept natural by the saving grace of error.
To lift, to fetch, to drive, to shed, to pen
Are acts I recognize, with all they mean
Of shepherding the unruly, for a kind of
Controlled woolgathering is my work too.

C. DAY LEWIS

83 Stupidity Street

I saw with open eyes
Singing birds sweet
Sold in the shops
For the people to eat,
Sold in the shops of
Stupidity Street.

I saw in vision
The worm in the wheat,
And in the shops nothing
For people to eat;
Nothing for sale in
Stupidity Street.

RALPH HODGSON

84 The Poor Man's Pig

Already fallen plum-bloom stars the green,
  And apple-boughs as knarred as old toads' backs
Wear their small roses ere a rose is seen;
  The building thrush watches old Job who stacks
The bright-peeled osiers on the sunny fence;
  The pent sow grunts to hear him stumping by,
And tries to push the bolt and scamper thence,
  But her ringed snout still keeps her to the sty.

Then out he lets her run; away she snorts
  In building gallop for the cottage door,
With hungry hubbub begging crusts and orts,
  Then like a whirlwind bumping round once more;
Nuzzling the dog, making the pullets run,
And sulky as a child when her play's done.

EDMUND BLUNDEN

85 **View of a Pig**

The pig lay on a barrow dead.
It weighed, they said, as much as three men.
Its eyes closed, pink white eyelashes.
Its trotters stuck straight out.

Such weight and thick pink bulk
Set in death seemed not just dead.
It was less than lifeless, further off.
It was like a sack of wheat.

I thumped it without feeling remorse.
One feels guilty insulting the dead,
Walking on graves. But this pig
Did not seem able to accuse.

It was too dead. Just so much
A poundage of lard and pork
Its last dignity had entirely gone.
It was not a figure of fun.

Too dead now to pity.
To remember its life, din, stronghold
Of earthly pleasure as it had been,
Seemed a false effort, and off the point.

Too deadly factual. Its weight
Oppressed me – how could it be moved?
And the trouble of cutting it up!
The gash in its throat was shocking, but not pathetic.

Once I ran at a fair in the noise
To catch a greased piglet
That was faster and nimbler than a cat,
Its squeal was the rending of metal.

Pigs must have hot blood, they feel like ovens.
Their bite is worse than a horse's –
They chop a half-moon clean out.
They eat cinders, dead cats.

Distinctions and admirations such
As this one was long finished with.
I stared at it a long time. They were going to
scald it,
Scald it and scour it like a doorstep.

TED HUGHES

86 At Grass

The eye can hardly pick them out
From the cold shade they shelter in,
Till wind distresses tail and mane;
Then one crops grass, and moves about
– The other seeming to look on –
And stands anonymous again.

Yet fifteen years ago, perhaps
Two dozen distances sufficed
To fable them: faint afternoons
Of Cups and Stakes and Handicaps,
Whereby their names were artificed
To inlay faded, classic Junes –

Silks at the start: against the sky
Numbers and parasols: outside,
Squadrons of empty cars, and heat,
And littered grass: then the long cry
Hanging unhushed till it subside
To stop-press columns on the street.

Do memories plague their ears like flies?
They shake their heads. Dusk brims the shadows.
Summer by summer all stole away,
The starting-gates, the crowds and cries –
All but the unmolesting meadows.
Almanacked, their names live; they

Have slipped their names, and stand at ease,
Or gallop for what must be joy,
And not a field-glass sees them home,
Or curious stop-watch prophesies:
Only the groom, and the groom's boy,
With bridles in the evening come.

PHILIP LARKIN

87 Hedgehog

Twitching the leaves just where the drainpipe clogs
In ivy leaves and mud, a purposeful
Creature at night about its business. Dogs
Fear his stiff seriousness. He chews away

At beetles, worms, slugs, frogs. Can kill a hen
With one snap of his jaws, can taunt a snake
To death on muscled spines. Old countrymen
Tell tales of hedgehogs sucking a cow dry.

But this one, cramped by houses, fences, walls,
Must have slept here all winter in that heap
Of compost, or have inched by intervals
Through tidy gardens to this ivy bed.

And here, dim-eyed, but ears so sensitive
A voice within the house can make him freeze,
He scuffs the edge of danger: yet can live
Happily in our nights and absences.

A country creature, wary, quiet and shrewd,
He takes the milk we give him, when we're gone.
At night our slamming voices must seem crude
To one who sits and waits for silences.

ANTHONY THWAITE

88 An Otter

Underwater eyes, an eel's
Oil of water body, neither fish nor beast is the otter:
Four-legged yet water-gifted, to outfish fish;
With webbed feet and long ruddering tail
And a round head like an old tomcat.

Brings the legend of himself
From before wars or burials, in spite of hounds and
vermin-poles;
Does not take root like the badger. Wanders, cries;
Gallops along land he no longer belongs to;
Re-enters the water by melting.

Of neither water nor land. Seeking
Some world lost when first he dived, that he cannot
come at since,
Takes his changed body into the holes of lakes;
As if blind, cleaves the stream's push till he licks
The pebbles of the source; from sea

To sea crosses in three nights
Like a king in hiding. Crying to the old shape of the
starlit land,
Over sunken farms where the bats go round,
Without answer. Till light and birdsong come
Walloping up roads with the milk wagon.

TED HUGHES

89 On a Favourite Cat, Drowned in a Tub of Goldfishes

'Twas on a lofty vase's side,
Where China's gayest art had dyed
  The azure flowers that blow,
Demurest of the tabby kind,
The pensive Selima, reclined,
  Gazed on the lake below.

Her conscious tail her joy declared:
The fair round face, the snowy beard,
  The velvet of her paws,
Her coat that with the tortoise vies,
Her ears of jet, and emerald eyes,
  She saw; and purred applause.

Still had she gazed, but 'midst the tide
Two angel forms were seem to glide,
  The Genii of the stream:
Their scaly armour's Tyrian hue
Through richest purple to the view
  Betrayed a golden gleam.

The hapless Nymph with wonder saw:
A whisker first, and then a claw
  With many an ardent wish
She stretched, in vain, to reach the prize –
What female heart can gold despise?
  What Cat's averse to Fish?

Presumptuous maid! with looks intent
Again she stretched, again she bent,
  Nor knew the gulf between –
Malignant Fate sat by and smiled –
The slippery verge her feet beguiled;
  She tumbled headlong in!

Eight times emerging from the flood
She mewed to every watery God
  Some speedy aid to send: –
No Dolphin came, no Nereid stirred,
Nor cruel Tom nor Susan heard –
  A favourite has no friend!

From hence, ye Beauties, undeceived,
Know one false step is ne'er retrieved,
  And be with caution bold:
Not all that tempts your wandering eyes
And heedless hearts, is lawful prize,
  Nor all that glisters, gold!

THOMAS GRAY

90 Milk for the Cat

When the tea is brought at five o'clock,
And all the neat curtains are drawn with care,
The little black cat with bright green eyes
Is suddenly purring there.

At first she pretends, having nothing to do,
She has come in merely to blink by the grate,
But, though tea may be late or the milk may be sour,
She is never late.

And presently her agate eyes
Take a soft large milky haze,
And her independent casual glance
Becomes a stiff hard gaze.

Then she stamps her claws or lifts her ears,
Or twists her tail and begins to stir,
Till suddenly all her lithe body becomes
One breathing trembling purr.

The children eat and wriggle and laugh;
The two old ladies stroke their silk;
But the cat is grown small and thin with desire,
Transformed to a creeping lust for milk.

The white saucer like some full moon descends
At last from the clouds of the table above;
She sighs and dreams and thrills and glows,
Transfigured with love.

She nestles over the shining rim,
Buries her chin in the creamy sea;
Her tail hangs loose; each drowsy paw
Is doubled under each bended knee.

A long dim ecstasy holds her life;
Her world is an infinite shapeless white,
Till her tongue has curled the last holy drop,
Then she sinks back into the night,

Draws and dips her body to heap
Her sleepy nerves in the great arm-chair,
Lies defeated and buried deep
Three or four hours unconscious there.

HAROLD MONRO

91 London Tom-Cat

Look at the gentle savage, monstrous gentleman
With jungles in his heart, yet metropolitan
As we shall never be; who – while his human hosts,
Afraid of their own past and its primaeval ghosts,
Pile up great walls for comfort – walks coquettishly
Through their elaborate cares, sure of himself and free
To be like them, domesticated, or aloof!
A dandy in the room, a demon on the roof,
He's delicately tough, endearingly reserved,
Adaptable, fastidious, rope-and-fibre-nerved.
Now an accomplished Yogi good at sitting still
He ponders ancient mysteries on the window-sill,
Now stretches, bares his claws and saunters off to find
The thrills of love and hunting, cunningly combined.
Acrobat, diplomat, and simple tabby cat,
He conjures tangled forests in a furnished flat.

MICHAEL HAMBURGER

92 Apartment Cats

The Girls wake, stretch, and pad up to the door.
They rub my leg and purr:
One sniffs around my shoe,
Rich with an outside smell,
The other rolls back on the floor –
White bib exposed, and stomach of soft fur.

Now, more awake, they re-enact Ben Hur
Along the corridor,
Gallop, wheel; as they do,
Their noses twitching still,
Their eyes get wild, their bodies tense,
Their usual prudence seemingly withdraws.

And then they wrestle: parry, lock of paws,
Blind hug of close defence,
Tail-thump, and smothered mew.
If either, though, feel claws,
She abruptly rises, knowing well
How to stalk off in wise indifference.

THOM GUNN

93 Kangaroo

In the northern hemisphere
Life seems to leap at the air, or skim under the wind
Like stags on rocky ground, or pawing horses, or
  spring scut-tailed rabbits.

Or else rush horizontal to charge at the sky's horizon,
Like bulls or bisons or wild pigs.

Or slip like water slippery towards its ends,
As foxes, stoats, and wolves, and prairie dogs.

Only mice, and moles, and rats, and badgers, and
  beavers, and perhaps bears
Seem belly-plumbed to the earth's mid-navel.
Or frogs that when they leap come flop, and flop to
  the centre of the earth.

But the yellow antipodal Kangaroo, when she sits up,
Who can unseat her, like a liquid drop that is heavy,
  and just touched earth?
The downward drip.
The down-urge.
So much denser than cold-blooded frogs.

Delicate mother Kangaroo
Sitting up there rabbit-wise, but huge, plumb-weighted,
And lifting her beautiful slender face, oh! so much
  more gently and finely lined than a rabbit's, or than
  a hare's,
Lifting her face to nibble at a round white peppermint
  drop, which she loves, sensitive mother Kangaroo.

Her sensitive, long, pure-bred face.
Her full antipodal eyes, so dark,
So big and quiet and remote, having watched so many empty dawns in silent Australia.

Her little loose hands, and drooping Victorian shoulders.
And then her great weight below the waist, her vast pale belly
With a thin young yellow little paw hanging out, and straggle of a thin long ear, like ribbon,
Like a funny trimming to the middle of her belly, thin little dangle of an immature paw, and one thin ear.

Her belly, her big haunches
And, in addition, the great muscular python stretch of her tail.

There, she shan't have any more peppermint drops.
So she wistfully, sensitively sniffs the air, and then turns and goes off in slow sad leaps
On the long flat skis of her legs,
Steered and propelled by that steel-strong snake of a tail.

Stops again, half turns, inquisitive to look back.
While something stirs quickly in her belly, and a lean little face comes out, as from a window,
Peaked, and a bit dismayed,
Only to disappear again quickly away from the sight of the world, to snuggle down in the warmth,
Leaving the trail of a different paw hanging out.

Still she watches with eternal, cocked wistfulness!
How full her eyes are, like the full fathomless,
shining eyes of an Australian black-boy
Who has been lost so many centuries on the margins
of existence!

She watches with insatiable wistfulness.
Untold centuries of watching for something to come,
For a new signal from life, in that silent lost land of
the South.

Where nothing bites but insects and snakes and the
sun, small life.
Where no bull roared, no cow ever lowed, no stag
cried, no leopard screeched, no lion coughed, no
dog barked,
But all was silent except for parrots occasionally, in
the haunted blue bush.

Wistfully watching, with wonderful liquid eyes.
And all her weight, all her blood, dripping sack-wise
down towards the earth's centre.
And the live little one taking in its paw at the door
of her belly.

Leap then, and come down on the line that draws to
the earth's deep, heavy centre.

D. H. LAWRENCE

94 The Tiger

Tiger, tiger, burning bright
In the forests of the night,
What immortal hand or eye
Could frame thy fearful symmetry?

In what distant deeps or skies
Burnt the fire of thine eyes?
On what wings dare he aspire?
What the hand dare seize the fire?

And what shoulder, and what art,
Could twist the sinews of thy heart?
And when thy heart began to beat,
What dread hand? and what dread feet?

What the hammer? what the chain?
In what furnace was thy brain?
What the anvil? what dread grasp
Dare its deadly terrors clasp?

When the stars threw down their spears,
And watered heaven with their tears,
Did He smile His work to see?
Did He who made the lamb make thee?

Tiger, tiger, burning bright
In the forests of the night,
What immortal hand or eye
Dare frame thy fearful symmetry?

WILLIAM BLAKE

95 Au Jardin des Plantes

The gorilla lay on his back,
One hand cupped under his head,
Like a man.

Like a labouring man tired with work,
A strong man with his strength burnt away
In the toil of earning a living.

Only of course he was not tired out with work,
Merely with boredom; his terrible strength
All burnt away by prodigal idleness.

A thousand days, and then a thousand days,
Idleness licked away his beautiful strength,
He having no need to earn a living.

It was all laid on, free of charge.
We maintained him, not for doing anything,
But for being what he was.

And so that Sunday morning he lay on his back,
Like a man, like a worn-out man,
One hand cupped under his terrible hard head.

Like a man, like a man,
One of those we maintain, not for doing anything,
But for being what they are.

A thousand days, and then a thousand days,
With everything laid on, free of charge,
They cup their heads in prodigal idleness.

JOHN WAIN

96 **Snake**

A snake came to my water-trough
On a hot, hot day, and I in pyjamas for the heat,
To drink there.

In the deep, strange-scented shade of the great dark
  carob-tree
I came down the steps with my pitcher
And must wait, must stand and wait, for there he was
  at the trough before me.

He reached down from a fissure in the earthwall in
  the gloom
And trailed his yellow-brown slackness soft-bellied
  down, over the edge of the stone trough
And rested his throat upon the stone bottom,

And where the water had dripped from the tap,
in a small clearness,
He sipped with his straight mouth,
Softly drank through his straight gums, into his
slack long body,
Silently.

Someone was before me at my water-trough,
And I, like a second comer, waiting.

He lifted his head from his drinking, as cattle do,
And looked at me vaguely, as drinking cattle do,
And flickered his two-forked tongue from his lips,
and mused a moment,
And stopped and drank a little more,
Being earth-brown, earth-golden from the burning
bowels of the earth
On the day of Sicilian July, with Etna smoking.

The voice of my education said to me
He must be killed,
For in Sicily the black, black snakes are innocent,
the gold are venomous.

And voices in me said, If you were a man
You would take a stick and break him now, and
finish him off.

But I must confess how I liked him,
How glad I was he had come like a guest in quiet, to
drink at my water-trough
And depart peaceful, pacified, and thankless,
Into the burning bowels of this earth.

Was it cowardice, that I dared not kill him?
Was it perversity, that I longed to talk to him?
Was it humility, to feel so honoured?
I felt so honoured.

And yet those voices:
If you were not afraid, you would kill him!

And truly I was afraid, I was most afraid,
But even so, honoured still more
That he should seek my hospitality
From out the dark door of the secret earth.

He drank enough
And lifted his head, dreamily, as one who has drunken,
And flickered his tongue like a forked night on
  the air, so black,
Seeming to lick his lips,
And looked around like a god, unseeing, into the air,
And slowly turned his head,
And slowly, very slowly, as if thrice adream,
Proceeded to draw his slow length curving round
And climb again the broken bank of my wall-face.

And as he put his head into that dreadful hole,
And as he slowly drew up, snake-easing his
  shoulders, and entered farther,
A sort of horror, a sort of protest against his
  withdrawing, into that horrid black hole,
Deliberately going into the blackness, and
  slowly drawing himself after,
Overcame me now his back was turned.

I looked round, I put down my pitcher,
I picked up a clumsy log
And threw it at the water-trough with a clatter.

I think it did not hit him,
But suddenly that part of him that was left
behind convulsed in undignified haste,
Writhed like lightning, and was gone
Into the black hole, the earth-lipped fissure in the
wall-front,
At which, in the intense still noon, I stared with
fascination.

And immediately I regretted it.
I thought how paltry, how vulgar, what a mean act!
I despised myself and the voices of my accursed
human education.

And I thought of the albatross,
And I wished he would come back, my snake.

For he seemed to me again like a king,
Like a king in exile, uncrowned in the underworld,
Now due to be crowned again.

And so, I missed my chance with one of the lords
Of life.
And I have something to expiate;
A pettiness.

D. H. LAWRENCE

97 **Bat**

At evening, sitting on this terrace,
When the sun from the west, beyond Pisa, beyond the
  mountains of Carrara
Departs, and the world is taken by surprise . . .

When the tired flower of Florence is in gloom beneath
  the glowing
Brown hills surrounding . . .

When under the arches of the Ponte Vecchio
A green light enters against stream, flush from the
west,
Against the current of obscure Arno . . .

Look up, and you see things flying
Between the day and the night;
Swallows with spools of dark thread sewing the
shadows together.

A circle swoop, and a quick parabola under the bridge
arches
Where light pushes through;
A sudden turning upon itself of a thing in the air.
A dip to the water.

And you think:
"The swallows are flying so late!"

Swallows?

Dark air-life looping
Yet missing the pure loop . . .
A twitch, a twitter, an elastic shudder in flight
And serrated wings against the sky,
Like a glove, a black glove thrown up at the light,
And falling back.

Never swallows!
Bats!
The swallows are gone.

At a wavering instant the swallows give way to bats
By the Ponte Vecchio . . .
Changing guard.

Bats, and an uneasy creeping in one's scalp
As the bats swoop overhead!
Flying madly.

Pipistrello!
Black piper on an infinitesimal pipe.
Little lumps that fly in air and have voices indefinite,
   wildy vindictive;

Wings like bits of umbrella.

Bats!

Creatures that hang themselves up like an old rag, to
   sleep;
And disgustingly upside down.
Hanging upside down like rows of disgusting old rags
And grinning in their sleep.

Bats!

In China the bat is symbol of happiness.

Not for me!

D. H. LAWRENCE

The poet's business is not to describe *things to us, or to tell us about things, but to create in our minds the very things themselves.*

Lascelles Abercrombie

98 Feeding Ducks

One duck stood on my toes.
The others made watery rushes after bread
Thrown by my momentary hand; instead
She stood duck-still and got far more than those.

An invisible drone boomed by
With a beetle in it; the neighbour's yearning bull
Bugled across five fields. And an evening full
Of other evenings quietly began to die.

And my everlasting hand
Dropped on my hypocrite duck her grace of bread.
And I thought, "The first to be fattened, the first to be
dead,"
Till my gestures enlarged, wide over the darkening
land.

NORMAN MACCAIG

99 I Heard a Linnet Courting

I heard a linnet courting
  His lady in the spring:
His mates were idly sporting,
  Nor stayed to hear him sing
    His song of love. –
I fear my speech distorting
    His tender love.

The phrases of his pleading
  Were full of young delight;
And she that gave him heeding
  Interpreted aright
    His gay, sweet notes, –
So sadly marred in the reading, –
    His tender notes.

And when he ceased, the hearer
  Awaited the refrain,
Till swiftly perching nearer
  He sang his song again,
    His pretty song: –
Would that my verse spake clearer
    His tender song!

Ye happy, airy creatures!
  That in the merry spring
Think not of what misfeatures
  Or cares the year may bring;
    But unto love
Resign your simple natures,
    To tender love.

ROBERT BRIDGES

100 The Linnet

Upon this leafy bush
  With thorns and roses in it,
Flutters a thing of light,
  A twittering linnet,
And all the throbbing world
  Of dew and sun and air
By this small parcel of life
  Is made more fair;
As if each bramble-spray
  And mounded gold-wreathed furze,
Harebell and little thyme,
  Were only hers;
As if this beauty and grace
  Did to one bird belong,
And, at a flutter of wing,
  Might vanish in song.

WALTER DE LA MARE

101 The Green Linnet

Beneath these fruit-tree boughs that shed
Their snow-white blossoms on my head,
With brightest sunshine round me spread
  Of spring's unclouded weather,
In this sequestered nook how sweet
To sit upon my orchard-seat!
And birds and flowers once more to greet,
  My last year's friends together.

One have I marked, the happiest guest
In all this covert of the blest:
Hail to thee, far above the rest
  In joy of voice and pinion!
Thou, Linnet! in thy green array,
Presiding spirit here to-day,
Dost lead the revels of the May,
  And this is thy dominion.

While birds, and butterflies, and flowers,
Make all one band of paramours,
Thou, ranging up and down the bowers,
  Art sole in thy employment;
A life, a presence like the air,
Scattering thy gladness without care,
Too blest with any one to pair,
  Thyself thy own enjoyment.

Amid yon tuft of hazel-trees,
That twinkle to the gusty breeze,
Behold him perched in ecstasies,
  Yet seeming still to hover;
There! where the flutter of his wings
Upon his back and body flings
Shadows and sunny glimmerings,
  That cover him all over.

My dazzled sight he oft deceives –
A brother of the dancing leaves;
Then flits, and from the cottage-eaves
  Pours forth his song in gushes;
As if by that exulting strain
He mocked and treated with disdain
The voiceless form he chose to feign,
  While fluttering in the bushes.

WILLIAM WORDSWORTH

102 **Curlew**

Dropped from the air at evening, this desolate call
Mocks us, who listen to its delicate non-humanity.
Dogs smile, cats flatter, cows regard us all
With eyes like those of ladies in a city,

So that we transfer to them familiar human virtues
To comfort and keep us safe. But this adamant bird
With the plaintive throat and curved, uneasy jaws
Crying creates a desert with a word

More terrible than chaos, and we stand at the edge
Of nothing. How shall we know its purpose, this
  wild bird,
Whose world is not confined by the linnet's hedge,
Whose mouth lets fly the appalling cry we heard?

LESLIE NORRIS

103 **Lapwing**

Leaves, summer's coinage spent, are all together
whirled,
sent spinning, dipping, slipping, shuffled by heavy-
handed wind,
shifted sideways, sifted, lifted, and in swarms made
to fly
spent sun-flies, gorgeous tatters, airdrift, pinions of
trees.

Pennons of the autumn wind, flying the same loose
flag,
minions of the rush of air, companions of draggled
cloud,
tattered, scattered pell-mell, diving, with side-slip
suddenly wailing
as they scale the uneasy sky flapping the lapwing fly.

Plover, with under the tail pine-red, dead leaf-wealth
in down displayed,
crested with glancing crests, sheeny with seagreen,
mirror of movement
of the deep sea horses plunging, restless, fretted by the
whip of wind,
tugging green tons, wet waste, lugging a mass to
Labrador.

See them fall wailing over high hill tops with hue and
cry,
like uneasy ghosts slipping in the dishevelled air,

with ever so much of forlorn ocean and wastes of wind
in their elbowing of the air and in their lamentable call.

R. E. WARNER

104 The Lakeside, Corsham

A stern swan, his neck a question,
Swam to me out of the liquid sun
That lapped the listening water on
The wild talk of a quiet stone.
He appeared to listen at the lake's deep brim.

Long and alone in the dim
Undercover cavern of the leaves'
Reflecting, green-lapping eaves,
I leaned, over and under the moving waves.
Nothing was wearing the water's gloves.

Over the lake top's brilliant graves
A bird's note, like a stone knocking,
Was knocked on a stone, starting, stopping.
The tapping water fluttered with coupling
Lights on the sun-riddled leaves overlapping.

In washes of green over green overlapping
On nothing but evening melting the flake of the moon.
– Then in the darkling air of the lake's deep swoon,
Gravely pondered, swam serenely away with the sun
Of an answered question, silent, a swan.

JAMES KIRKUP

105 The Wild Swans at Coole

The trees are in their autumn beauty,
The woodland paths are dry,
Under the October twilight the water
Mirrors a still sky;
Upon the brimming water among the stones
Are nine-and-fifty swans.

The nineteenth Autumn has come upon me
Since I first made my count;
I saw, before I had well finished,
All suddenly mount
And scatter wheeling in great broken rings
Upon their clamorous wings.

I have looked upon those brilliant creatures,
And now my heart is sore.
All's changed since I, hearing at twilight,
The first time on this shore,
The bell-beat of their wings above my head,
Trod with a lighter tread.

Unwearied still, lover by lover,
They paddle in the cold,
Companionable streams or climb the air;
Their hearts have not grown old;
Passion or conquest, wander where they will,
Attend upon them still.

But now they drift on the still water
Mysterious, beautiful;
Among what rushes will they build,
By what lake's edge or pool
Delight men's eyes when I awake some day
To find they have flown away?

W. B. YEATS

106 **Cuckoos**

When coltsfoot withers and begins to wear
Long silver locks instead of golden hair,
And fat red catkins from black poplars fall
And on the ground like caterpillars crawl,
And bracken lifts up slender arms and wrists
And stretches them, unfolding sleepy fists,
The cuckoos in a few well-chosen words
Tell they give Easter eggs to the small birds.

ANDREW YOUNG

107 To the Cuckoo

O blithe new-comer! I have heard,
I hear thee and rejoice:
O Cuckoo! shall I call thee Bird,
Or but a wandering Voice?

While I am lying on the grass
Thy twofold shout I hear;
From hill to hill it seems to pass,
At once far off and near.

Though babbling only to the vale
Of sunshine and of flowers,
Thou bringest unto me a tale
Of visionary hours.

Thrice welcome, darling of the Spring!
Even yet thou art to me
No bird, but an invisible thing,
A voice, a mystery;

The same whom in my schoolboy days
I listened to; that cry
Which made me look a thousand ways
In bush, and tree, and sky.

To seek thee did I often rove
Through woods and on the green;
And thou wert still a hope, a love;
Still longed for, never seen!

And I can listen to thee yet;
  Can lie upon the plain
And listen, till I do beget
  That golden time again.

O blessèd bird! the earth we pace
  Again appears to be
An unsubstantial, faery place,
  That is fit home for thee.

WILLIAM WORDSWORTH

108 **The Jackdaw**

There is a bird, who by his coat,
And by the hoarseness of his note,
  Might be supposed a crow;
A great frequenter of the church,
Where bishop-like he finds a perch,
  And dormitory too.

Above the steeple shines a plate,
That turns and turns, to indicate
  From what point blows the weather:
Look up – your brains begin to swim,
'Tis in the clouds – that pleases him,
  He chooses it the rather.

Fond of the speculative height,
Thither he wings his airy flight,
And thence securely sees
The bustle and the raree-show
That occupy mankind below,
Secure and at his ease.

You think, no doubt, he sits and muses
On future broken bones and bruises,
If he should chance to fall.
No; not a single thought like that
Employs his philosophic pate,
Or troubles it at all.

He sees that this great roundabout,
The world, with all its motley rout,
Church, army, physic, law,
Its customs, and its businesses,
Is no concern at all of his,
And says – what says he? – Caw.

Thrice happy bird! I too have seen
Much of the vanities of men;
And, sick of having seen 'em,
Would cheerfully these limbs resign
For such a pair of wings as thine,
And such a head between 'em.

WILLIAM COWPER

109 **Thames Gulls**

Beautiful it is to see
On London Bridge the bold-eyed seabirds wheel,
And hear them cry, and all for a light-flung crust
Fling us their wealth, their freedom, speed and gleam.
And beautiful to see
Them that pass by lured by these birds to stay,
And smile and say "how tame they are" – how tame!
Friendly as stars to steersmen in mid seas,
And as remote as midnight's darling stars,
Pleasant as voices heard from days long done,
As nigh the hand as windflowers in the woods,
And inaccessible as Dido's phantom.

EDMUND BLUNDEN

110 **The Owl**

When cats run home and light is come,
  And dew is cold upon the ground,
And the far-off stream is dumb,
  And the whirring sail goes round,
  And the whirring sail goes round:
    Alone and warming his five wits,
    The white owl in the belfry sits.

When merry milkmaids click the latch,
  And rarely smells the new-mown hay,
And the cock hath sung beneath the thatch
  Twice or thrice his roundelay,
  Twice or thrice his roundelay:
    Alone and warming his five wits,
    The white owl in the belfry sits.

ALFRED TENNYSON

111 **Disturbances**

After the darkness has come
And the distant planes catch fire
In the dusk, coming home,
And the tall church spire
No longer stands on the hill
And the streets are quiet except
For a car-door slamming – well,
You might say the houses slept.
An owl calls from a tree.

This is my house and home,
A place where for several years
I've settled, to which I've come
Happily, set my shears
To the hedge which fronts the place,
Had decorators in,
Altered a former face
To a shape I can call my own.
An owl calls from a tree.

Only, sometimes at night
Or running downhill for a train,
I suddenly catch sight
Of a world not named and plain
And without hedges or walls:
A jungle of noises, fears,
No lucid intervals,
No calm exteriors.
An owl calls from a tree.

The place I live in has
A name on the map, a date
For all that is or was.
I avoid hunger and hate:
I have a bed for the night:
The dishes are stacked in the rack:
I remember to switch off the light:
I turn and lie on my back.
An owl calls from a tree.

ANTHONY THWAITE

112 Town Owl

On eves of cold, when slow coal fires,
rooted in basements, burn and branch,
brushing with smoke the city air;

When quartered moons pale in the sky
and neons glow along the dark
like deadly nightshade on a briar;

Above the muffled traffic then
I hear the owl, and at his note
I shudder in my private chair.

For like an augur he has come
to roost among our crumbling walls,
his blooded talons sheathed in fur.

Some secret lure of time it seems
has called him from his country wastes
to hunt a newer wasteland here.

And where the candelabra swung,
bright with the dancers' thousand eyes,
now his black, hooded pupils stare,

And where the silk-shoed lovers ran
with dust of diamonds in their hair,
he opens now his silent wing,

And, like a stroke of doom, drops down,
and swoops across the empty hall,
and plucks a quick mouse off the stair . . .

LAURIE LEE

113 **The Owl**

Downhill I came, hungry, and yet not starved;
Cold, yet had heat within me that was proof
Against the North wind; tired, yet so that rest
Had seemed the sweetest thing under a roof.

Then at the inn I had food, fire, and rest,
Knowing how hungry, cold, and tired was I.
All of the night was quite barred out except
An owl's cry, a most melancholy cry

Shaken out long and clear upon the hill,
No merry note, nor cause of merriment,
But one telling me plain what I escaped
And others could not, that night, as in I went.

And salted was my food, and my repose,
Salted and sobered, too, by the bird's voice
Speaking for all who lay under the stars,
Soldiers and poor, unable to rejoice.

EDWARD THOMAS

114 **Ode to a Nightingale**

My heart aches, and a drowsy numbness pains
  My sense, as though of hemlock I had drunk,
Or emptied some dull opiate to the drains
  One minute past, and Lethe-wards had sunk:
'Tis not through envy of thy happy lot,
  But being too happy in thy happiness,
    That thou, light-wingèd Dryad of the trees,
      In some melodious plot
  Of beechen green, and shadows numberless,
    Singest of summer in full-throated ease.

O for a draught of vintage! that hath been
  Cooled a long age in the deep-delvèd earth,
Tasting of Flora and the country-green,
  Dance, and Provençal song, and sunburnt mirth!
O for a beaker full of the warm South,
  Full of the true, the blushful Hippocrene,
    With beaded bubbles winking at the brim,
      And purple-stainèd mouth;
  That I might drink, and leave the world unseen,
    And with thee fade away into the forest dim:

Fade far away, dissolve, and quite forget
  What thou among the leaves has never known,
The weariness, the fever, and the fret
  Here, where men sit and hear each other groan;
Where palsy shakes a few, sad, last grey hairs,
  Where youth grows pale, and spectre-thin, and dies;
    Where but to think is to be full of sorrow
      And leaden-eyed despairs;

Where beauty cannot keep her lustrous eyes,
Or new Love pine at them beyond to-morrow.

Away! away! for I will fly to thee,
Not charioted by Bacchus and his pards,
But on the viewless wings of Poesy,
Though the dull brain perplexes and retards;
Already with thee! tender is the night,
And haply the Queen-Moon is on her throne,
Clustered around by all her starry Fays;
But here there is no light,
Save what from heaven is with the breezes blown
Through verdurous glooms and winding mossy ways.

I cannot see what flowers are at my feet,
Nor what soft incense hangs upon the boughs,
But, in embalmèd darkness, guess each sweet
Wherewith the seasonable month endows
The grass, the thicket, and the fruit-tree wild;
White hawthorn, and the pastoral eglantine;
Fast-fading violets covered up in leaves;
And mid-May's eldest child,
The coming musk-rose, full of dewy wine,
The murmurous haunt of flies on summer eves.

Darkling I listen; and for many a time
I have been half in love with easeful Death,
Called him soft names in many a musèd rhyme,
To take into the air my quiet breath;
Now more than ever seems it rich to die,
To cease upon the midnight with no pain,

While thou art pouring forth thy soul abroad
In such an ecstasy!
Still wouldst thou sing, and I have ears in vain –
To thy high requiem become a sod.

Thou wast not born for death, immortal Bird!
No hungry generations tread thee down;
Thy voice I hear this passing night was heard
In ancient days by emperor and clown:
Perhaps the self-same song that found a path
Through the sad heart of Ruth, when, sick for home,
She stood in tears amid the alien corn;
The same that oft-times hath
Charmed magic casements, opening on the foam
Of perilous seas, in faery lands forlorn.

Forlorn! the very word is like a bell
To toll me back from thee to my sole self!
Adieu! the fancy cannot cheat so well
As she is famed to do, deceiving elf.
Adieu! adieu! thy plaintive anthem fades
Past the near meadows, over the still stream,
Up the hill-side; and now 'tis buried deep
In the next valley-glades:
Was it a vision, or a waking dream?
Fled is that music: – do I wake or sleep?

JOHN KEATS

115 The Nightingale near the House

Here is the soundless cypress on the lawn:
It listens, listens. Taller trees beyond
Listen. The moon at the unruffled pond
  Stares. And you sing, you sing.

That star-enchanted song falls through the air
From lawn to lawn down terraces of sound,
Darts in white arrows on the shadowed ground;
  While all the night you sing.

My dreams are flowers to which you are a bee,
As all night long I listen, and my brain
Receives your song, then loses it again
  In moonlight on the lawn.

Now is your voice a marble high and white,
Then like a mist on fields of paradise;
Now is a raging fire, then is like ice,
  Then breaks, and it is dawn.

HAROLD MONRO

116 To the Nightingale

O nightingale, that on yon bloomy spray
  Warblest at eve, when all the woods are still,
  Thou with fresh hope the lover's heart doth fill
  While the jolly hours lead on propitious May.
Thy liquid notes that close the eye of day,
  First heard before the shallow cuckoo's bill,
  Portend success in love; oh, if Jove's will
  Have linked that amorous power to thy soft lay,
Now timely sing, ere the rude bird of hate
  Foretell my hopeless doom in some grove nigh,
  As thou from year to year hast sung too late
For my relief, yet hadst no reason why.
  Whether the Muse, or Love, call thee his mate,
  Both of them I serve, and of their train am I.

JOHN MILTON

117 **The Swallows**

All day – when early morning shone
With every dewdrop its own dawn
And when cockchafers were abroad
Hurtling like missiles that had lost their road –

The swallows twisting here and there
Round unseen corners of the air
Upstream and down so quickly passed
I wondered that their shadows flew as fast.

They steeple-chased over the bridge
And dropped down to a drowning midge
Sharing the river with the fish,
Although the air itself was their chief dish.

Blue-winged snowballs! until they turned
And then with ruddy breasts they burned;
All in one instant everywhere,
Jugglers with their own bodies in the air.

ANDREW YOUNG

118 The Thrush's Nest

Within a thick and spreading hawthorn bush,
That overhung a molehill large and round,
I heard from morn to morn a merry thrush
Sing hymns to sunrise, and I drank the sound
With joy; and, often an intruding guest,
I watched her secret toils from day to day, –
How true she warped the moss to form a nest,
And modelled it within with wood and clay;
And by and by, like heath-bells gilt with dew,
There lay her shining eggs, as bright as flowers,
Ink-spotted-over, shells of greeny blue;
And there I witnessed, in the sunny hours,
A brood of Nature's minstrels chirp and fly,
Glad as that sunshine and the laughing sky.

JOHN CLARE

119 **The Ecstatic**

Lark, skylark, spilling your rubbed and round
Pebbles of sound in air's still lake,
Whose widening circles fill the noon; yet none
Is known so small beside the sun:

Be strong your fervent soaring, your skyward air!
Tremble there, a nerve of song!
Float up there where voice and wing are one,
A singing star, a note of light!

Buoyed, embayed in heaven's noon-wide reaches –
For soon light's tide will turn – oh stay!
Cease not till day streams to the west, then down
That estuary drop down to peace.

C. DAY LEWIS

120 **The Gentle Lark** (From *Venus and Adonis*)

Lo, here the gentle lark, weary of rest,
From his moist cabinet mounts up on high,
And wakes the morning, from whose silver breast
The sun ariseth in his majesty;
  Who doth the world so gloriously behold,
  That cedar-tops and hills seem burnished gold.

WILLIAM SHAKESPEARE

121 A Blackbird Singing

It seems wrong that out of this bird,
Black, bold, a suggestion of dark
Places about it, there yet should come
Such rich music, as though the notes'
Ore were changed to a rare metal
At one touch of that bright bill.

You have heard it often, alone at your desk
In a green April, your mind drawn
Away from its work by sweet disturbance
Of the mild evening outside your room.

A slow singer, but loading each phrase
With history's overtones, love, joy
And grief learned by his dark tribe
In other orchards and passed on
Instinctively as they are now,
But fresh always with new tears.

R. S. THOMAS

122 **Chough**

Desolate that cry as though world were unworthy.
See now, rounding the headland, a forlorn hopeless
  bird,
trembling black wings fingering the blowy air,
dainty and ghostly, careless of the scattering salt.

This is the cave-dweller that flies like a butterfly,
buffeted by daws, almost extinct, who has chosen,
so gentle a bird, to live on furious coasts.

Here where sea whistles in funnels, and slaps the backs
of burly granite slabs and hisses over holes,
in bellowing hollows that shelter the female seal
the Cornish chough wavers over the waves.

By lion rocks, rocks like the heads of queens,
sailing with ragged plumes upturned, into the wind
goes delicate indifferent the doomed bird.

R. E. WARNER

123 The Eagle

He clasps the crag with crooked hands;
Close to the sun in lonely lands,
Ringed with the azure world, he stands.

The wrinkled sea beneath him crawls;
He watches from his mountain walls,
And like a thunderbolt he falls.

ALFRED TENNYSON

124 The Unknown Bird

Three lovely notes he whistled, too soft to be heard
If others sang; but others never sang
In the great beech-wood all that May and June.
No one saw him: I alone could hear him
Though many listened. Was it but four years
Ago? or five? He never came again.

Oftenest when I heard him I was alone,
Nor could I ever make another hear.
La-la-la! he called seeming far-off –
As if a cock crowed past the edge of the world,
As if the bird or I were in a dream.
Yet that he travelled through the trees and
  sometimes
Neared me, was plain, though somehow distant still
He sounded. All the proof is – I told men
What I had heard.

I never knew a voice,
Man, beast, or bird, better than this. I told
The naturalists; but neither had they heard
Anything like the notes that did so haunt me,
I had them clear by heart and have them still.
Four years, or five, have made no difference. Then
As now that La-la-la! was bodiless sweet:
Sad more than joyful it was, if I must say
That it was one or other, but if sad
'Twas sad only with joy too, too far off
For me to taste it. But I cannot tell
If truly never anything but fair
The days were when he sang, as now they seem.
This surely I know, that I who listened then,
Happy sometimes, sometimes suffering
A heavy body and a heavy heart,
Now straightway, if I think of it, become
Light as that bird wandering beyond my shore.

EDWARD THOMAS

125 **The Birds**

Brother thrush it was began
Matins for the dawn of man.
Brother Falcon watched him climb
Blindly from the depths of time,
Watched him till the earth, and bend
Fire and water to his end.
Brother Eagle, over all,
Heard the towering forests fall,
Saw the cities come and go
On the shifting world below.

Brother Gull, suspended there
On the noiseless waves of air,
Saw him ride the waves of sea
Buoyantly, triumphantly.
Brother Plover heard him rise
Thunderous toward the skies,
Saw the smooth projectiles follow
Brother Hawk and Brother Swallow,
And the mushroom cloudbursts grow
On the wasted world below.

Rooks in their high parliament
Say men to destruction sent
Bird and beast and fish, and then
Turned their hatred on to men,
Till they squandered equally
Air and fire, land and sea;
But, they say, when ages on
Men and all their works have gone,
Brother Lark will sing for them
His exultant Requiem.

CLIVE SANSOM

Poetry is the language in which man explores his own amazement.

Christopher Fry

126 **Travel**

I should like to rise and go
Where the golden apples grow;
Where below another sky
Parrot islands anchored lie,
And, watched by cockatoos and goats,
Lonely Crusoes building boats;

Where in the sunshine reaching out
Eastern cities, miles about,
Are with mosque and minaret
Among sandy gardens set,
And the rich goods from near and far
Hang for sale in the bazaar;

Where the Great Wall round China goes,
And on one side the desert blows,
And with bell and voice and drum,
Cities on the other hum;
Where are forests, hot as fire,
Wide as England, tall as a spire,
Full of apes and coco-nuts
And the negro hunters' huts;

Where the knotty crocodile
Lies and blinks in the Nile,
And the red flamingo flies
Hunting fish before his eyes;
Where in jungles, near and far,
Man-devouring tigers are,

Lying close and giving ear
Lest the hunt be drawing near,
Or a comer-by be seen
Swinging in a palanquin;

Where among the desert sands
Some deserted city stands,
All its children, sweep and prince,
Grown to manhood ages since,
Not a foot in street or house,
Not a stir of child or mouse,
And when kindly falls the night,
In all the town no spark of light.

There I'll come when I'm a man
With a camel caravan;
Light a fire in the gloom
Of some dusty dining-room;
See the pictures on the walls,
Heroes, fights, and festivals;
And in a corner find the toys
Of the old Egyptian boys.

ROBERT LOUIS STEVENSON

127 **Travelling Between Places**

Leaving nothing and nothing ahead;
when you stop for the evening
the sky will be in ruins,

when you hear late birds
with tired throats singing
think how good it is that they,

knowing you were coming,
stayed up late to greet you
who travels between places

when the late afternoon
drifts into the woods, when
nothing matters specially.

BRIAN PATTEN

128 **Tewkesbury Road**

It is good to be out on the road, and going one knows not where,
Going through meadow and village, one knows not whither nor why;
Through the grey light drift of the dust, in the keen cool rush of the air,
Under the flying white clouds, and the broad blue lift of the sky.

And to halt at the chattering brook, in the tall green fern at the brink
Where the harebell grows, and the gorse, and the foxgloves purple and white;
Where the shy-eyed delicate deer come down in a troop to drink
When the stars are mellow and large at the coming on of the night.

O, to feel the beat of the rain, and the homely smell of the earth,
Is a tune for the blood to jig to, a joy past power of words;
And the blessèd green comely meadows are all a-ripple with mirth
At the noise of the lambs at play and the dear wild cry of the birds.

JOHN MASEFIELD

129 **The Vagabond**

Give to me the life I love,
  Let the lave go by me,
Give the jolly heaven above
  And the by-way nigh me.
Bed in the bush with stars to see –
  Bread I dip in the river –
There's the life for a man like me,
  There's the life for ever.

Let the blow fall soon or late,
  Let what will be o'er me;
Give the face of earth around
  And the road before me.
Wealth I seek not, hope nor love,
  Nor a friend to know me;
All I seek, the heaven above
  And the road below me.

Or let autumn fall on me
  Where afield I linger,
Silencing the bird on tree,
  Biting the blue finger.
White as meal the frosty field –
  Warm the fireside haven –
Not to autumn will I yield,
  Not to winter even!

Let the blow fall soon or late,
  Let what will be o'er me;
Give the face of earth around
  And the road before me.
Wealth I ask not, hope nor love,
  Nor a friend to know me;
All I ask, the heaven above
  And the road below me.

ROBERT LOUIS STEVENSON

130 **Journey of the Magi**

"A cold coming we had of it,
Just the worst time of the year
For a journey, and such a long journey:
The ways deep and the weather sharp,
The very dead of winter."
And the camels galled, sore-footed, refractory,
Lying down in the melting snow.
There were times we regretted
The summer palaces on slopes, the terraces,
And the silken girls bringing sherbet.
Then the camel men cursing and grumbling
And running away, and wanting their liquor and women,
And the night-fires going out, and the lack of shelters,
And the cities hostile and the towns unfriendly
And the villages dirty and charging high prices:
A hard time we had of it.
At the end we preferred to travel all night,
Sleeping in snatches,
With the voices singing in our ears, saying
That this was all folly.

Then at dawn we came down to a temperate valley,
Wet, below the snow line, smelling of vegetation;
With a running stream and a water-mill beating the darkness,
And three trees on the low sky.
And an old white horse galloped away in the meadow.
Then we came to a tavern with vine-leaves over the lintel,

Six hands at an open door dicing for pieces of silver,
And feet kicking the empty wine-skins.
But there was no information, and so we continued
And arrived at evening, not a moment too soon
Finding the place; it was (you may say) satisfactory.

All this was a long time ago, I remember,
And I would do it again, but set down
This set down
This: were we led all that way for
Birth or Death? There was a Birth, certainly,
We had evidence and no doubt. I had seen birth and death,
But had thought they were different; this Birth was
Hard and bitter agony for us, like Death, our death.
We turned to our places, these Kingdoms,
But no longer at ease here, in the old dispensation,
With an alien people clutching their gods.
I should be glad of another death.

T. S. ELIOT

131 How They Brought the Good News from Ghent to Aix

I sprang to the stirrup, and Joris, and he;
I galloped, Dirck galloped, we galloped all three;
"Good speed!" cried the watch, as the gate-bolts
  undrew;
"Speed!" echoed the wall to us galloping through;
Behind shut the postern, the lights sank to rest,
And into the midnight we galloped abreast.

Not a word to each other; we kept the great pace
Neck by neck, stride by stride, never changing our
  place;
I turned in my saddle, and made its girths tight,
Then shortened each stirrup, and set the pique right,
Rebuckled the cheek-strap, chained slacker the bit,
Nor galloped less steadily Roland a whit.

'Twas moonset at starting; but while we drew near
Lokeren' the cocks crew and twilight dawned clear;
At Boom, a great yellow star came out to see;
At Düffield 'twas morning as plain as could be;
And from Mecheln church-steeple we heard the half-
  chime,
So Joris broke silence with, "Yet there is time!"

At Aerschot, up leaped of a sudden the sun,
And against him the cattle stood black every one,
To stare through the mist at us galloping past,
And I saw my stout galloper Roland at last
With resolute shoulders, each butting away
The haze, as some bluff river headland its spray!

And his low head and crest, just one sharp ear bent
  back
For my voice, and the other pricked out on his track;
And one eye's black intelligence, – ever that glance
O'er its white edge at me, his own master, askance!
And the thick heavy spume flakes which aye and anon
His fierce lips shook upwards in galloping on.

By Hasselt, Dirck groaned; and cried Joris, "Stay spur!
Your Roos galloped bravely, the fault's not in her.
We'll remember at Aix" – for one heard the quick
  wheeze
Of her chest, saw the stretched neck and staggering
  knees,
And sunk tail, and horrible heave of the flank,
As down on her haunches she shuddered and sank.

So we were left galloping, Joris and I,
Past Looz and past Tongres, no cloud in the sky;
The broad sun above laughed a pitiless laugh,
'Neath our feet broke the brittle bright stubble-like
  chaff;
Till over by Dalhem a dome-spire sprang white,
And "Gallop," gasped Joris, "for Aix is in sight!"

"How they'll greet us!" – and all in a moment his roan
Rolled neck and croup over, lay dead as a stone:
And there was my Roland to bear the whole weight
Of the news which alone could save Aix from her fate,
With his nostrils like pits full of blood to the brim,
And with circles of red for his eye-sockets' rim.

Then I cast loose my buffcoat, each holster let fall,
Shook off both my jack-boots, let go belt and all,
Stood up in the stirrup, leaned, patted his ear,
Called my Roland his pet-name, my horse without
  peer;
Clapped my hands, laughed and sang, any noise, bad
  or good,
Till at length into Aix Roland galloped and stood.

And all I remember is – friends flocking round
As I sat with his head 'twixt my knees on the ground,
And no voice but was praising this Roland of mine,
As I poured down his throat our last measure of wine,
Which (the burgesses voted by common consent)
Was no more than his due who brought good news
  from Ghent.

ROBERT BROWNING

132 **The Cyclist**

Freewheeling down the escarpment past the unpassing
horse
Blazoned in chalk the wind he causes in passing
Cools the sweat of his neck, making him one with the
sky,
In the heat of the handlebars he grasps the summer
Being a boy and to-day a parenthesis

Between the horizon's brackets; the main sentence
Is to be picked up later but these five minutes
Are all to-day and summer. The dragonfly
Rises without take-off, horizontal,
Underlining itself in a sliver of peacock light.

And glaring, glaring white
The horse on the down moves within his brackets,
The grass boils with grasshoppers, a pebble
Scutters from under the wheel and all this country
Is spattered white with boys riding their heat-wave,
Feet on a narrow plank and hair thrown back

And a surf of dust beneath them. Summer, summer –
They chase it with butterfly nets or strike it into the
   deep
In a little red ball or gulp it lathered with cream
Or drink it through closed eyelids; until the bell
Left-right-left gives his forgotten sentence
And reaching the valley the boy must pedal again
Left-right-left but meanwhile
For ten seconds more can move as the horse in the
   chalk
Moves unbeginningly calmly
Calmly regardless of tenses and final clauses
Calmly unendingly moves.

LOUIS MACNEICE

P.S.—G

133 **Morning Express**

Along the wind-swept platform, pinched and white,
The travellers stand in pools of wintry light,
Offering themselves to morn's long, slanting arrows.
The train's due; porters trundle laden barrows.
The train steams in, volleying resplendent clouds
Of sun-blown vapour. Hither and about,
Scared people hurry, storming the doors in crowds.
The officials seem to waken with a shout,
Resolved to hoist and plunder; some to the vans
Leap; others rumble the milk in gleaming cans.
Boys, indolent-eyed, from baskets leaning back,
Question each face; a man with a hammer steals
Stooping from coach to coach; with clang and clack,
Touches and tests, and listens to the wheels.
Guard sounds a warning whistle, points to the clock
With brandished flag, and on his folded flock
Claps the last door: the monster grunts: "Enough!"
Tightening his load of links with pant and puff.
Under the arch, then forth into blue day,
Glide the processional windows on their way,
And glimpse the stately folk who sit at ease
To view the world like kings taking the seas
In prosperous weather: drifting banners tell
Their progress to the counties; with them goes
The clamour of their journeying; while those
Who sped them stand to wave a last farewell.

SIEGFRIED SASSOON

134 **Night Mail**

This is the night mail crossing the border,
Bringing the cheque and the postal order,
Letters for the rich, letters for the poor,
The shop at the corner and the girl next door.
Pulling up Beattock, a steady climb –
The gradient's against her, but she's on time.

Past cotton grass and moorland boulder,
Shovelling white steam over her shoulder,
Snorting noisily as she passes
Silent miles of wind-bent grasses.
Birds turn their heads as she approaches,
Stare from the bushes at her blank-faced coaches.
Sheepdogs cannot turn her course,
They slumber on with paws across.
In the farm she passes no one wakes,
But a jug in the bedroom gently shakes.

Dawn freshens, the climb is done.
Down towards Glasgow she descends
Towards the steam tugs yelping down the glade of
  cranes,
Towards the fields of apparatus, the furnaces
Set on the dark plain like gigantic chessmen.
All Scotland waits for her:
In the dark glens, beside the pale-green lochs,
Men long for news.

Letters of thanks, letters from banks,
Letters of joy from girl and boy,
Receipted bills, and invitations
To inspect new stock or visit relations,
And applications for situations
And timid lovers' declarations
And gossip, gossip from all the nations,
News circumstantial, news financial,
Letters with holiday snaps to enlarge in,
Letters with faces scrawled in the margin,

Letters from uncles, cousins and aunts,
Letters to Scotland from the South of France,
Letters of condolence to Highlands and Lowlands,
Notes from overseas to Hebrides
Written on paper of every hue,
The pink, the violet, the white and the blue,
The chatty, the catty, the boring, adoring,
The cold and official and the heart's outpouring,
Clever, stupid, short and long,
The typed and the printed and the spelt all wrong.

Thousands are still asleep
Dreaming of terrifying monsters,
Or a friendly tea beside the band at Cranston's or
Crawford's,
Asleep in working Glasgow, asleep in well-set
Edinburgh,
Asleep in granite Aberdeen.
They continue their dreams;
But shall wake soon and long for letters,
And none will hear the postman's knock
Without a quickening of the heart,
For who can hear and feel himself forgotten?

W. H. AUDEN

135 **Sleeping Compartment**

I don't like this, being carried sideways
Through the night. I feel wrong and helpless – like
A timber broadside in a fast stream.

Such a way of moving may suit
That odd snake the sidewinder
In Arizona: but not me in Perthshire.

I feel at rightangles to everything,
A crossgrain in existence. – It scrapes
The top of my head, my footsoles.

To forget outside is no help either –
Then I become a blockage
In the long gut of the train.

I try to think I am a through-the-looking-glass
Mountaineer bivouacked
On a ledge five feet high.

It's no good. I go sidelong.
I rock sideways. . . . I draw in my feet
To let Aviemore pass.

NORMAN MACCAIG

136 **Casey Jones**

Come all you rounders if you want to hear
The story of a brave engineer;
Casey Jones was the hogger's name,
On a big eight-wheeler, boys, he won his fame.
Caller called Casey at half-past four,
He kissed his wife at the station door,
Mounted to the cabin with orders in his hand,
And took his farewell trip to the promised land.

Casey Jones, he mounted to the cabin,
Casey Jones, with his orders in his hand!
Casey Jones, he mounted to the cabin,
Took his farewell trip into the promised land.

Put in your water and shovel in your coal,
Put your head out the window, watch the drivers roll,
I'll run her till she leaves the rail,
'Cause we're eight hours late with the Western Mail!
He looked at his watch and his watch was slow,
Looked at the water and the water was low,
Turned to his fireboy and said,
"We'll get to 'Frisco, but we'll all be dead!"

Casey Jones, he mounted to the cabin,
Casey Jones, with his orders in his hand!
Casey Jones, he mounted to the cabin,
Took his farewell trip into the promised land.

Casey Jones pulled up Reno Hill,
Tooted for the crossing with an awful shrill,
Snakes all knew by the engine's moans
That the hogger at the throttle was Casey Jones.
He pulled up short two miles from the place,
Number Four stared him right in the face,
Turned to his fireboy, said "You'd better jump,
'Cause there's two locomotives going to bump!"

Casey Jones, he mounted to the cabin,
Casey Jones, with his orders in his hand!
Casey Jones, he mounted to the cabin,
Took his farewell trip into the promised land.

Casey said, just before he died,
"There's two more roads I'd like to ride."
Fireboy said, "What can they be?"
"The Rio Grande and the Old S.P."
Mrs. Jones sat on her bed a-sighing,
Got a pink that Casey was dying,
Said "Go to bed, children; hush your crying,
'Cause you'll get another papa on the Salt Lake line."

Casey Jones! Got another papa!
Casey Jones, on the Salt Lake Line!
Casey Jones! Got another papa!
Got another papa on the Salt Lake Line!

ANONYMOUS

137 From a Railway Carriage

Faster than fairies, faster than witches,
Bridges and houses, hedges and ditches;
And charging along like troops in a battle,
All through the meadows the houses and cattle;
And all of the sights of the hill and the plain
Fly as thick as driving rain;
And ever again, in the wink of an eye,
Painted stations whistle by.

Here is a child who clambers and scrambles,
All by himself and gathering brambles;
Here is a tramp who stands and gazes;
And here is the green for stringing the daisies!
Here is a cart run away in the road
Lumping along with man and load;
And here is a mill, and there is a river;
Each a glimpse and gone for ever!

ROBERT LOUIS STEVENSON

138 **Here Live Your Life Out!**

Window-gazing, at one time or another
In the course of travel, you must have startled at
Some coign of true felicity. "Stay!" it beckoned,
"Here live your life out!" If you were simple-hearted
The village rose, perhaps, from a broad stream
Lined with alders and gold-flowering flags –
Hills, hay-fields, orchards, mills – and, plain to see,
The very house behind its mulberry-tree
Stood, by a miracle, untenanted!

Alas, you could not alight, found yourself jolted
Viciously on; public conveyances
Are not amenable to casual halts
Except in sternly drawn emergencies –
Bandits, floods, landslides, earthquakes or the like –
Nor could you muster resolution enough
To shout: "This is emergency, let me out!",
Rushing to grasp their brakes; so the whole scene
Withdrew for ever. Once at the terminus
(As your internal mentor will have told you),
It would have been pure folly to engage
A private car, drive back, sue for possession.
Too far, too late:
Already bolder tenants were at the gate.

ROBERT GRAVES

139 Adlestrop

Yes. I remember Adlestrop –
The name, because one afternoon
Of heat the express-train drew up there
Unwontedly. It was late June.

The steam hissed. Someone cleared his throat.
No one left and no one came
On the bare platform. What I saw
Was Adlestrop – only the name

And willows, willow-herb, and grass,
And meadowsweet, and haycocks dry,
No whit less still and lonely fair
Than the high cloudlets in the sky.

And for that minute a blackbird sang
Close by, and round him, mistier,
Farther and farther, all the birds
Of Oxfordshire and Gloucestershire.

EDWARD THOMAS

140 The Express

After the first powerful plain manifesto
The black statement of pistons, without more fuss
But gliding like a queen, she leaves the station.
Without bowing and with restrained unconcern
She passes the houses which humbly crowd outside,
The gasworks, and at last the heavy page
Of death, printed by gravestones in the cemetery.
Beyond the town there lies the open country
Where, gathering speed, she acquires mystery,
The luminous self-possession of ships on ocean.
It is now she begins to sing – at first quite low
Then loud, and at last with a jazzy madness –
The song of her whistle screaming at curves,
Of deafening tunnels, brakes, innumerable bolts.
And always light, aerial, underneath,
Retreats the elate metre of her wheels.
Steaming through metal landscape on her lines,
She plunges new eras of wild happiness,
Where speed throws up strange shapes, broad curves
And parallels clean like the steel of guns.
At last, further than Edinburgh or Rome,
Beyond the crest of the world, she reaches night
Where only a low stream-line brightness
Of phosphorus on the tossing hills is white.
Ah, like a comet through flame she moves entranced,
Wrapt in her music no bird song, no, nor bough
Breaking with honey buds, shall ever equal.

STEPHEN SPENDER

141 **Seen from the Train**

Somewhere between Crewkerne
And Yeovil it was. On the left of the line
Just as the crinkled hills unroll
To the plain. A church on a small green knoll –
A limestone church,
And above the church
Cedar boughs stretched like hands that yearn
To protect or to bless. The whole

Stood up, antique and clear
As a cameo, from the vale. I swear
It was not a dream. Twice, thrice had I found it
Chancing to look as my train wheeled round it.
But this time I passed
Though I gazed as I passed
All the way down the valley, that knoll was not there,
Nor the church, nor the trees it mounded.

What came between to unsight me? . . .
But suppose, only suppose there might be
A secret look in a landscape's eye
Following you as you hasten by,
And you have your chance –
Two or three chances
At most – to hold and interpret it rightly,
Or it is gone for aye.

There was a time when men
Would have called it a vision, said that sin
Had blinded me since to a heavenly fact.
Well, I have neither invoked nor faked
Any church in the air,
And little I care
Whether or no I shall see it again.
But blindly my heart is racked

When I think how, not twice or thrice,
But year after year in another's eyes
I have caught the look that I missed today
Of the church, the knoll, the cedars – a ray
Of the faith, too, they stood for,
The hope they were food for,
The love they prayed for, facts beyond price –
And turned my eyes away.

C. DAY LEWIS

142 **A Local Train of Thought**

Alone, in silence, at a certain time of night,
Listening, and looking up from what I'm trying to
write,
I hear a local train along the Valley. And "There
Goes the one-fifty," think I to myself; aware
That somehow its habitual travelling comforts me,
Making my world seem safer, homelier, sure to be
The same to-morrow; and the same, one hopes, next
year.
"There's peacetime in that train." One hears it
disappear
With needless warning whistle and rail-resounding
wheels.
"That train's quite like an old familiar friend," one
feels.

SIEGFRIED SASSOON

143 **Above the Storm**

Sheer through the storm into the sun the plane
Shot, streaming silver from its wings;
And he who'd won through volleys of blind rain
And baffling smother of dense cloud
To heights of rare
And eager air,
Keen-edged as icy wine,
Where only man's heart sings
In the celestial hyaline,
Where only man's heart sings, adoring,
Beyond the range even of the eagle's soaring –
He, who had braved the tempest's rage and roaring,
Sang out above the loud
Propeller's whirring
As in the crystal light
Above the curded white
Of billowy snows.

He rose
Even to his own heart's height;
And happily in flashing flight
He soared and swooped
And zoomed and looped
With ease unerring
Through the unsearchable inane
In dizzy circles of insane
And death-defying insolence
Of youth's delight

Above the sunny dense
And seething cloud whereunder
Still rolled the thunder
Over an earth already drowned in night.

He soared and swooped again,
Exulting in the flawless enginery
Of hand and brain
That, even in the heady urgency
And wildest flight
Of his insatiable soul,
Obeying his intrepid will,
Still kept serene control
Of his frail plane
That hung
Ever on peril's edge and swung
In thin and scarce-sustaining air
As by a single hair,
When one missed heart-beat or untaken breath
Might lunge him in a fiery plunge to death.

And still in aerial ecstasy,
A flittering midge in the infinity
Of heaven, he revelled till the light
Drained even from that celestial height,
And through the icy beryl of the night
Star after star dawned silverly.

W. W. GIBSON

144 **The Astronaut**

Star-sailor, with your eyes on space,
You map an ocean in the sky at night.
I see you stride with scientific grace
Upon the crusted suns of yesterday
As if it were to-morrow, in the place
Of time, the voyager beyond this momentary stay
Whose loaded instruments of light
Shoot rocket-galaxies around the bend of sight.

JAMES KIRKUP

THE SEA

Poetry can communicate the actual quality of experience with a subtlety and precision approachable by no other means.

F. R. Leavis

145 Sea Fever

I must down to the seas again, to the lonely sea and
the sky,
And all I ask is a tall ship and a star to steer her by,
And the wheel's kick and the wind's song and the
white sail's shaking,
And a grey mist on the sea's face and a grey dawn
breaking.

I must down to the seas again, for the call of the
running tide
Is a wild call and a clear call that may not be denied;
And all I ask is a windy day with the white clouds
flying,
And the flung spray and the blown spume, and the
seagulls crying.

I must down to the seas again, to the vagrant gypsy
life,
To the gull's way and the whale's way where the
wind's like a whetted knife;
And all I ask is a merry yarn from a laughing fellow-
rover,
And quiet sleep and a sweet dream when the long
trick's over.

JOHN MASEFIELD

146 The Beach

Louder than gulls the little children scream
Whom fathers haul into the jovial foam;
But others fearlessly rush in, breast high,
Laughing the salty water from their mouths –
Heroes of the nursery.

The horny boatman, who has seen whales
And flying fishes, who has sailed as far
As Demerara and the Ivory Coast,
Will warn them, when they crowd to hear his tales,
That every ocean smells alike of tar.

ROBERT GRAVES

147 **Christmas at Sea**

The sheets were frozen hard, and they cut the naked
hand;
The decks were like a slide, where a seaman scarce
could stand;
The wind was a nor'wester, blowing squally off the
sea;
And cliffs and spouting breakers were the only things
a-lee.

They heard the surf a-roaring before the break of day;
But 'twas only with the peep of light we saw how ill
we lay.
We tumbled every hand on deck instanter, with a
shout,
And we gave her the maintops'l, and stood by to go
about.

All day we tacked and tacked between the South
  Head and the North;
All day we hauled the frozen sheets, and got no further
  forth;
All day as cold as charity, in bitter pain and dread,
For very life and nature we tacked from head to head.

We gave the South a wider berth, for there the tide-
  race roared;
But every tack we made we brought the North Head
  close aboard
So's we saw the cliffs and houses, and the breakers
  running high,
And the coastguard in his garden, with his glass against
  his eye.

The frost was on the village roofs as white as ocean
  foam;
The good red fires were burning bright in every
  longshore home;
The windows sparkled clear, and the chimneys volleyed
  out;
And I vow we sniffed the victuals as the vessel went
  about.

The bells upon the church were rung with a mighty
  jovial cheer;
For it's just that I should tell you how (of all days in
  the year)
This day of our adversity was blessèd Christmas morn,
And the house above the coastguard's was the house
  where I was born.

O well I saw the pleasant room, the pleasant faces
there,
My mother's silver spectacles, my father's silver hair;
And well I saw the firelight, like a flight of homely
elves,
Go dancing round the china-plates that stand upon the
shelves.

And well I knew the talk they had, the talk that was of
me,
Of the shadow on the household and the son that
went to sea;
And O the wicked fool I seemed, in every kind of way,
To be here and hauling frozen ropes on blessèd
Christmas Day.

They lit the high sea-light, and the dark began to fall.
"All hands to loose topgallant sails," I heard the
captain call.
"By the Lord she'll never stand it," our first mate,
Jackson, cried.
. . . "It's one way or the other, Mr. Jackson," he
replied.

She staggered to her bearings, but the sails were new
and good,
And the ship smelt up to windward just as though she
understood.
As the winter's day was ending, in the entry of the
night,
We cleared the weary headland and passed below the
light.

And they heaved a mighty breath, every soul on board
  but me,
As they saw her nose again pointing handsome out to
  sea;
But all that I could think of, in the darkness and the
  cold,
Was just that I was leaving home and my folks were
  growing old.

ROBERT LOUIS STEVENSON

148 A Passer-By

Whither, O splendid ship, thy white sails crowding,
  Leaning across the bosom of the urgent West,
That fearest nor sea rising, nor sky clouding,
  Whither away, fair rover, and what thy quest?
  Ah! soon, when Winter has all our vales opprest,
When skies are cold and misty, and hail is hurling,
  Wilt thou glide on the blue Pacific, or rest
In a summer haven asleep, thy white sails furling.

I there before thee, in the country that well thou
    knowest,
  Already arrived am inhaling the odorous air:
I watch thee enter unerringly where thou goest,
  And anchor queen of the strange shipping there,
  Thy sails for awnings spread, thy masts bare;
Nor is aught from the foaming reef to the snow-capped,
    grandest
  Peak, that is over the feathery palms, more fair
Than thou, so upright, so stately and still thou standest.

And yet, O splendid ship, unhailed and nameless,
  I know not if, aiming a fancy, I rightly divine
That thou hast a purpose joyful, a courage blameless,
  Thy port assured in a happier land than mine.
  But for all I have given thee, beauty enough is
    thine,
As thou, aslant with trim tackle and shrouding,
  From the proud nostril curve of a prow's line
  In the offing scatterest foam, thy white sails
    crowding.

ROBERT BRIDGES

149 **Losing a Sail**

By walls half-built (to bar the creeping tide),
A ruined church, a pewter-coloured sea,
Salt, stagnant ponds: the marram stalks are plied
Beneath a wind that snaps all withering stems;
Dusk blurs the sickle-contour of the bay
On which, far out, a thirty-footer skims.

Lightly the yacht is heeling to the sails;
Its underbelly shines in the last sun
As warmly sparkling as mackerel's scales
When it is dying. Loosened by a reef,
The white jib bellies out; the jib-sheet gone,
It whirls to the horizon like a leaf.

EDWARD LUCIE-SMITH

150 **The Discovery**

There was an Indian, who had known no change,
  Who strayed content along a sunlit beach
Gathering shells. He heard a sudden strange
  Commingled noise; looked up; and gasped for
    speech.
For in the bay, where nothing was before,
  Moved on the sea, by magic, huge canoes,
With bellying cloths on poles, and not one oar,
  And fluttering coloured signs and clambering crews.

And he, in fear, this naked man alone,
  His fallen hands forgetting all their shells,
His lips gone pale, knelt low behind a stone,
And stared, and saw, and did not understand,
  Columbus's doom-burdened caravels
    Slant to the shore, and all their seamen land.

J. C. SQUIRE

151 **Enchantment**

On this fawn-coloured shore
All delicately strewn,
Gold dust and gleaming shell,
White stone and blue stone,
Lie sweetly together whether
Eyes be to see them or none.

The air is gay with voices
Of children. The sun
Casts flowers of purple shadow
Before them as they run,
Blows clouds and blooms of shadow
Where the swift feet may run.

Onward the children race
To leap into the sea
That bubbles silver bright
In the lovely revelry
Of foam and limbs together
In a white revelry.

How grew that airy tumult
On shores that were so still,
That wind of flowers and shadows?
What art invisible
Made all that airy wonder,
At what enchanter's will?

Æ

152 **Look, Stranger, . . .**

Look, stranger, at this island now
The leaping light for your delight discovers,
Stand stable here
And silent be,
That through the channels of the ear
May wander like a river
The swaying sound of the sea.

Here at the small field's ending pause
Where the chalk wall falls to the foam, and its tall
  ledges
Oppose the pluck
And knock of the tide,
And the shingle scrambles after the suck-
  ing surf, and the gull lodges
A moment on its sheer side.

Far off like floating seeds the ships
Diverge on urgent voluntary errands;
And the full view
Indeed may enter
And move in memory as now these clouds do,
That pass the harbour mirror
And all the summer through the water saunter.

W. H. AUDEN

153 **The Rock Pool**

This is the sea. In these uneven walls
A wave lies prisoned. Far and far away
Outward to ocean, as the slow tide falls,
Her sisters through the capes that hold the bay
Dancing in lovely liberty recede.
Yet lovely in captivity she lies,
Filled with soft colours, where the waving weed
Moves gently and discloses to our eyes
Blurred shining veins of rock and lucent shells
Under the light-shot water; and here repose
Small quiet fish and dimly glowing bells
Of sleeping sea-anemones that close
Their tender fronds and will not now awake
Till on these rocks the waves returning break.

EDWARD SHANKS

154 **The Shell**

See what a lovely shell,
Small and pure as a pearl,
Lying close to my foot,
Frail, but a work divine,
Made so fairily well
With delicate spire and whorl.
How exquisitely minute,
A miracle of design.

What is it? a learned man
Could give it a clumsy name.
Let him name it who can,
The beauty would be the same.

The tiny cell is forlorn,
Void of the little living will
That made it stir on the shore.
Did he stand at the diamond door
Of his house in a rainbow frill?
Did he push when he was uncurled
A golden foot or a fairy horn
Through his dim water world?

Slight, to be crushed with a tap
Of my finger-nail on the sand,
Small, but a work divine,
Frail, but of force to withstand,
Year upon year, the shock

Of cataract seas that snap
The three-decker's oaken spine
Athwart the ledges of rock,
Here on the Breton strand!

ALFRED TENNYSON

155 The Feather

I stoop to gather a seabird's feather
Fallen on the beach,
Torn from a beautiful drifting wing;
What can I learn or teach,
Running my finger through the comb
And along the horny quill?
The body it was torn from
Gave out a cry so shrill,
Sailors looked from their white road
To see what help was there.
It dragged the winds to a drop of blood
Falling through drowned air,
Dropping from the sea-hawk's beak,
From frenzied talons sharp;
Now if the words they lost I speak
It must be to that harp
Under the strange, light-headed sea
That bears a straw of the nest.
Unless I make that melody,
How can the dead have rest?

Sheer from wide air to the wilderness
The victim fell, and lay;
The starlike bone is fathomless,
Lost among wind and spray.
This lovely, isolated thing
Trembles amid their sound.
I set my finger on the string
That spins the ages round.
But let it sleep, let it sleep
Where shell and stone are cast;
Its ecstasy the Furies keep,
For nothing here is past,
The perfect into night must fly;
On this the winds agree.
How could a blind rock satisfy
The hungers of the sea?

VERNON WATKINS

156 The Heron

The cloud-backed heron will not move:
He stares into the stream.
He stands unfaltering while the gulls
And oyster-catchers scream.
He does not hear, he cannot see
The great white horses of the sea,
But fixes eyes on stillness
Below their flying team.

How long will he remain, how long
Have the grey woods been green?
The sky and the reflected sky,
Their glass he has not seen,
But silent as a speck of sand
Interpreting the sea and land,
His fall pulls down the fabric
Of all that windy scene.

Sailing with clouds and woods behind,
Pausing in leisured flight,
He stepped, alighting on a stone,
Dropped from the stars of night.
He stood there unconcerned with day,
Deaf to the tumult of the bay,
Watching a stone in water,
A fish's hidden light.

Sharp rocks drive back the breaking waves,
Confusing sea with air.
Bundles of spray blown mountain-high
Have left the shingle bare.
A shipwrecked anchor wedged by rocks,
Loosed by the thundering equinox,
Divides the herded waters,
The stallion and his mare.

Yet no distraction breaks the watch
Of that time-killing bird.
He stands unmoving on the stone;
Since dawn he has not stirred.
Calamity about him cries,
But he has fixed his golden eyes
On water's crooked tablet,
On light's reflected word.

VERNON WATKINS

157 **The Echoing Cliff**

White gulls that sit and float,
Each on his shadow like a boat,
Sandpipers, oystercatchers
And herons, those grey stilted watchers,
From loch and corran rise,
And as they scream and squawk abuse
Echo from wooded cliff replies
So clearly that the dark pine boughs,
Where goldcrests flit
And owls in drowsy wisdom sit,
Are filled with sea-birds and their cries.

ANDREW YOUNG

158 **Boats at Night**

How lovely is the sound of oars at night
  And unknown voices, borne through windless air,
From shadowy vessels floating out of sight
  Beyond the harbour lantern's broken glare
To those piled rocks that make on the dark wave
  Only a darker stain. The splashing oars
Slide softly on as in an echoing cave
  And with the whisper of the unseen shores
Mingle their music, till the bell of night
  Murmurs reverberations low and deep
That droop towards the land in swooning flight
  Like whispers from the lazy lips of sleep.
The oars grow faint. Below the cloud-dim hill
The shadows fade and now the bay is still.

EDWARD SHANKS

9 LAUGHTER

Extract poetry from anything you please: it lies in everything and everywhere.

Gustave Flaubert

159 **Mrs. Reece Laughs**

Laughter, with us, is no great undertaking,
A sudden wave that breaks and dies in breaking.
Laughter, with Mrs. Reece, is much less simple:
It germinates, it spreads, dimple by dimple,
From small beginnings, things of easy girth,
To formidable redundancies of mirth.
Clusters of subterranean chuckles rise
And presently the circles of her eyes
Close into slits, and all the woman heaves
As a great elm with all its mounds of leaves
Wallows before the storm. From hidden sources
A mustering of blind volcanic forces
Takes her and shakes her till she sobs and gapes.
Then all that load of bottled mirth escapes
In one wild crow, a lifting of huge hands,
And creaking stays, a visage that expands
In scarlet ridge and furrow. Thence collapse,
A hanging head, a feeble hand that flaps
An apron-end to stir an air and waft
A steaming face . . . And Mrs. Reece has laughed.

MARTIN ARMSTRONG

160 **Matilda**

who told lies, and was burned to death

Matilda told such Dreadful Lies,
It made one Gasp and Stretch one's Eyes;
Her Aunt, who from her Earliest Youth,
Had kept a Strict Regard for Truth,
Attempted to Believe Matilda:
The effort very nearly killed her,
And would have done so, had not She
Discovered this Infirmity.
For once, towards the Close of Day,
Matilda, growing tired of play,
And finding she was left alone,
Went tiptoe to the Telephone
And summoned the Immediate Aid
Of London's Noble Fire-Brigade.
Within an hour the Gallant Band
Were pouring in on every hand,
From Putney, Hackney Downs and Bow.
With Courage high and Hearts a-glow,
They galloped, roaring through the Town,
"Matilda's House is Burning Down!"
Inspired by British Cheers and Loud
Proceeding from the Frenzied Crowd,
They ran their ladders through a score
Of windows on the Ball Room Floor;
And took Peculiar Pains to Souse
The Pictures up and down the House,

Until Matilda's Aunt succeeded
In showing them they were not needed;
And even then she had to pay
To get the Men to go away!

It happened that a few Weeks later
Her Aunt was off to the Theatre
To see that Interesting Play
The Second Mrs. Tanqueray.
She had refused to take her Niece
To hear that Entertaining Piece:
A Deprivation Just and Wise
To Punish her for Telling Lies.
That Night a Fire DID break out –
You should have heard Matilda Shout!
You should have heard her Scream and Bawl,
And throw the window up and call
To People passing in the Street –
(The rapidly increasing Heat
Encouraging her to obtain
Their confidence) – but all in vain!
For every time She shouted "Fire!"
They only answered "Little Liar!"
And therefore when her Aunt returned,
Matilda, and the House, were Burned.

HILAIRE BELLOC

161 **Adventures of Isabel**

Isabel met an enormous bear;
Isabel, Isabel, didn't care.
The bear was hungry, the bear was ravenous,
The bear's big mouth was cruel and cavernous.
The bear said, "Isabel, glad to meet you,
How do, Isabel, now I'll eat you!"
Isabel, Isabel, didn't worry;
Isabel didn't scream or scurry.
She washed her hands and she straightened her hair up,
Then Isabel quietly ate the bear up.

Once on a night as black as pitch
Isabel met a wicked old witch.
The witch's face was cross and wrinkled,
The witch's gums with teeth were sprinkled.

"Ho, ho, Isabel!" the old witch crowed,
"I'll turn you into an ugly toad!"
Isabel, Isabel, didn't worry;
Isabel didn't scream or scurry.
She showed no rage and she showed no rancour,
But she turned the witch into milk and drank her.

Isabel met a hideous giant,
Isabel continued self-reliant.
The giant was hairy, the giant was horrid,
He had one eye in the middle of his forehead.
"Good morning, Isabel," the giant said,
"I'll grind your bones to make my bread."
Isabel, Isabel, didn't worry;
Isabel didn't scream or scurry.
She nibbled the zwieback that she always fed off,
And when it was gone, she cut the giant's head off.

Isabel met a troublesome doctor,
He punched and poked till he really shocked her.
The doctor's talk was of coughs and chills,
And the doctor's satchel bulged with pills.
The doctor said unto Isabel,
"Swallow this, it will make you well."
Isabel, Isabel, didn't worry;
Isabel didn't scream or scurry.
She took those pills from the pill-concoctor,
And Isabel calmly cured the doctor.

OGDEN NASH

162 The Frog

Be kind and tender to the Frog,
  And do not call him names,
As "Slimy-Skin" or "Pollywog"
  Or likewise "Uncle James",
Or "Gape-a-grin", or "Toad-gone-wrong",
  Or "Billy Bandy-knees";
The frog is justly sensitive
  To epithets like these.

No animal will more repay
  A treatment kind and fair,
At least so lonely people say
Who keep a frog (and, by the way,
  They are extremely rare).

HILAIRE BELLOC

163 The Frog

What a wonderful bird the frog are!
When he stands he sit almost;
When he hop he fly almost.
He ain't got no sense hardly;
He ain't got no tail hardly either.
When he sit, he sit on what he ain't got almost.

ANONYMOUS

164 By Way of Preface

How pleasant to know Mr. Lear!
  Who has written such volumes of stuff!
Some think him ill-tempered and queer,
  But a few think him pleasant enough.

His mind is concrete and fastidious,
  His nose is remarkably big;
His visage is more or less hideous,
  His beard it resembles a wig.

He has ears and two eyes and ten fingers,
  Leastways if you reckon two thumbs;
Long ago he was one of the singers,
  But now he is one of the dumbs.

He sits in a beautiful parlour,
  With hundreds of books on the wall;
He drinks a great deal of marsala,
  But never gets tipsy at all.

He has many friends, laymen and clerical,
  Old Foss is the name of his cat:
His body is perfectly spherical,
  He weareth a runcible hat.

When he walks in a waterproof white,
  The children run after him so!
Calling out, "He's come out in his night-
  gown, that crazy old Englishman, oh!"

He weeps by the side of the ocean,
  He weeps on the top of the hill;
He purchases pancakes and lotion,
  And chocolate shrimps from the mill.

He reads but he cannot speak Spanish,
  He cannot abide ginger-beer;
Ere the days of his pilgrimage vanish,
  How pleasant to know Mr. Lear!

EDWARD LEAR

165 If You Have Seen

Good reader! if you e'er have seen,
  When Phoebus hastens to his pillow,
The mermaids, with their tresses green,
  Dancing upon the western billow:
If you have seen, at twilight dim,
When the lone spirit's vesper hymn
  Floats wild along the winding shore:
If you have seen, through mist of eve,
The fairy train their ringlets weave,
Glancing along the spangled green; –
  If you have seen all this and more,
God bless me! what a deal you've seen!

THOMAS MOORE

166 The Priest and the Mulberry Tree

Did you hear of the curate who mounted his mare,
And merrily trotted along to the fair?
Of creature more tractable none ever heard:
In the height of her speed she would stop at a word;
But again with a word, when the curate said, "Hey,"
She put forth her mettle and galloped away.

As near to the gates of the city he rode,
While the sun of September all brilliantly glowed,
The good priest discovered, with eyes of desire,
A mulberry tree in a hedge of wild brier;
On boughs long and lofty, in many a green shoot,
Hung large, black, and glossy the beautiful fruit.

The curate was hungry and thirsty to boot;
He shrank from the thorns, though he longed for the
fruit;
With a word he arrested his courser's keen speed,
And he stood up erect on the back of his steed;
On the saddle he stood while the creature stood still,
And he gathered the fruit till he took his good fill.

"Sure never," he thought, "was a creature so rare,
So docile, so true, as my excellent mare;
Lo, here now I stand," and he gazed all around,
"As safe and as steady as if on the ground;
Yet how had it been, if some traveller this way,
Had, dreaming no mischief, but chanced to cry 'Hey'?"

He stood with his head in the mulberry tree,
And he spoke out aloud in his fond reverie;
At the sound of the word the good mare made a push,
And down went the priest in the wild-brier bush.
He remembered too late, on his thorny green bed,
Much that well may be thought cannot wisely be said.

THOMAS LOVE PEACOCK

167 **The Owl and the Pussy-Cat**

The Owl and the Pussy-Cat went to sea
In a beautiful pea-green boat,
They took some honey, and plenty of money,
Wrapped up in a five-pound note.
The Owl looked up to the stars above,
And sang to a small guitar,
"O lovely Pussy! O Pussy, my love,
What a beautiful Pussy you are,
  You are,
  You are!
What a beautiful Pussy you are!"

Pussy said to the Owl, "You elegant fowl!
How charmingly sweet you sing!
O let us be married! Too long we have tarried:
But what shall we do for a ring?"
They sailed away for a year and a day,
To the land where the Bong-tree grows,
And there in a wood a Piggy-wig stood,
With a ring at the end of his nose,
His nose,
His nose,
With a ring at the end of his nose.

"Dear Pig, are you willing to sell for one shilling
Your ring?" Said the Piggy, "I will."
So they took it away, and were married next day
By the Turkey who lives on the hill.
They dined on mince, and slices of quince,
Which they ate with a runcible spoon;
And hand in hand, on the edge of the sand,
They danced by the light of the moon,
The moon,
The moon,
They danced by the light of the moon.

EDWARD LEAR

168 An Elegy on the Death of a Mad Dog

Good people all, of every sort,
  Give ear unto my song;
And if you find it wondrous short,
  It cannot hold you long.

In Islington there was a man,
  Of whom the world might say,
That still a godly race he ran
  Whene'er he went to pray.

A kind and gentle heart he had,
  To comfort friends and foes;
The naked every day he clad,
  When he put on his clothes.

And in that town a dog was found,
  As many dogs there be,
Both mongrel, puppy, whelp, and hound,
  And curs of low degree.

This dog and man at first were friends;
  When a pique began,
The dog, to gain his private ends,
  Went mad and bit the man.

Around from all the neighbouring streets,
  The wondering neighbours ran,
And swore the dog had lost his wits,
  To bite so good a man.

The wound it seemed both sore and sad
  To every Christian eye:
And while they swore the dog was mad,
  They swore the man would die.

But soon a wonder came to light,
  That showed the rogues they lied,
The man recovered of the bite,
  The dog it was that died.

OLIVER GOLDSMITH

169 **I Had a Hippopotamus**

I had a hippopotamus; I kept him in a shed
And fed him upon vitamins and vegetable bread;
I made him my companion on many cheery walks,
And had his portrait done by a celebrity in chalks.

His charming eccentricities were known on every side,
The creature's popularity was wonderfully wide;
He frolicked with the Rector in a dozen friendly
  tussles.
Who could not but remark upon his hippopotamuscles.

If he should be afflicted by depressions or the dumps,
By hippopotameasles or the hippopotamumps,
I never knew a particle of peace till it was plain
He was hippotamasticating properly again.

I had a hippopotamus; I loved him as a friend;
But beautiful relationships are bound to have an end;
Time takes, alas! our joys from us and robs us of our
  blisses;
My hippopotamus turned out a hippopotamissis.

My housekeeper regarded him with jaundice in her
  eye;
She did not want a colony of hippopotami;
She borrowed a machine-gun from her soldier-nephew
  Percy,
And showed my hippopotamus no hippopotamercy.

My house now lacks the glamour that the charming
creature gave,
The garage where I kept him is as silent as a grave;
No longer he displays among the motor-tyres and
spanners
His hippopotamastery of hippopotamanners.

No longer now he gambols in the orchards in the
Spring;
No longer do I lead him through the village on a
string;
No longer in the mornings does the neighbourhood
rejoice
To his hippopotamusically-modulated voice.

I had a hippopotamus; but nothing upon earth
Is constant in its happiness or lasting in its mirth;
No joy that life can give me can be strong enough to
smother
My sorrow for what might-have-been-a-hippo-
potamother.

PATRICK BARRINGTON

Macavity's a Mystery Cat: he's called the Hidden Paw –
For he's the master criminal who can defy the Law.
He's the bafflement of Scotland Yard, the Flying Squad's despair:
For when they reach the scene of crime – Macavity's not there!

Macavity, Macavity, there's no one like Macavity,
He's broken every human law, he breaks the law of gravity.
His powers of levitation would make a fakir stare,
And when you reach the scene of crime Macavity's not there!
You may seek him in the basement, you may look up in the air –
But I tell you once and once again, Macavity's not there!

Macavity's a ginger cat, he's very tall and thin;
You would know him if you saw him, for his eyes are sunken in.
His brow is deeply lined with thought, his head is slightly domed;
His coat is dusty from neglect, his whiskers are uncombed.
He sways his head from side to side, with movements like a snake;
And when you think he's half asleep, he's always wide awake.

Macavity, Macavity, there's no one like Macavity,
For he's a fiend in feline shape, a monster of depravity.
You may meet him in a by-street, you may see him in
  the square –
But when a crime's discovered, then Macavity's not
  there!

He's outwardly respectable. (They say he cheats at
  cards.)
And his footprints are not found in any file of Scotland
  Yard's.
And when the larder's looted, or the jewel-case is rifled,
Or when the milk is missing, or another Peke's been
  stifled,
Or the greenhouse glass is broken, and the trellis past
  repair –
Ay, there's the wonder of the thing! Macavity's not
  there!

And when the Foreign Office finds a Treaty's gone
  astray,
Or the Admiralty lose some plans and drawings by the
  way,
There may be a scrap of paper in the hall or on the
  stair –
But it's useless to investigate – Macavity's not there!
And when the loss has been disclosed, the Secret Service
  say:
"It must have been Macavity!" – but he's a mile away.
You'll be sure to find him resting, or a-licking of his
  thumbs,
Or engaged in doing complicated long division sums.

Macavity, Macavity, there's no one like Macavity,
There never was a Cat of such deceitfulness and
suavity.
He always has an alibi, and one or two to spare:
At whatever time the deed took place – Macavity
wasn't there!
And they say that all the Cats whose wicked deeds are
widely known
(I might mention Mungojerrie, I might mention
Griddle-bone)
Are nothing more than agents for the Cat who all the
time
Just controls their operations: the Napoleon of Crime.

T. S. ELIOT

171 Gus: The Theatre Cat

Gus is the Cat at the Theatre Door.
His name, as I ought to have told you before,
Is really Asparagus. That's such a fuss
To pronounce, that we usually call him just Gus.
His coat's very shabby, he's thin as a rake,
And he suffers from palsy that makes his paw shake.
Yet he was, in his youth, quite the smartest of Cats –
But no longer a terror to mice and to rats.
For he isn't the Cat that he was in his prime;
Though his name was quite famous, he says, in its time.

And whenever he joins his friends at their club
(Which takes place at the back of the neighbouring
pub)
He loves to regale them, if someone else pays,
With anecdotes drawn from his palmiest days.
For he once was a star of the highest degree –
He has acted with Irving, he's acted with Tree,
And he likes to relate his success on the Halls,
Where the Gallery once gave him seven cat-calls,
But his grandest creation, as he loves to tell,
Was Firefrorefiddle, the Fiend of the Fell.

"I have played," so he says, "every possible part,
And I used to know seventy speeches by heart.
I'd extemporize back-chat, I knew how to gag,
And I knew how to let the cat out of the bag.
I knew how to act with my back and my tail;
With an hour of rehearsal, I never could fail.
I'd a voice that would soften the hardest of hearts,
Whether I took the lead, or in character parts.
I have sat by the bedside of poor Little Nell;
When the Curfew was rung, then I swung on the bell.
In the Pantomime season, I never fell flat,
And once understudied Dick Whittington's Cat.
But my grandest creation, as history will tell,
Was Firefrorefiddle, the Fiend of the Fell."

Then, if someone will give him a toothful of gin,
He will tell how he once played a part in
East Lynne.
At a Shakespeare performance he once walked on pat,
When some actor suggested the need for a cat.

He once played a Tiger – could do it again –
Which an Indian Colonel pursued down a drain.
And he thinks that he still can, much better than
 most,
Produce blood-curdling noises to bring on the Ghost.
And he once crossed the stage on a telegraph wire,
To rescue a child when a house was on fire.
And he says: "Now, these kittens, they do not get
 trained
As we did in the days when Victoria reigned.
They never get drilled in a regular troupe,
And they think they are smart, just to jump through
 a hoop."
And he'll say, as he scratches himself with his claws,
"Well, the Theatre's certainly not what it was.
These modern productions are all very well,
But there's nothing to equal, from what I hear tell,
 That moment of mystery
 When I made history
As Firefrorefiddle, the Fiend of the Fell."

T. S. ELIOT

172 **Father William**

"You are old, Father William," the young man said,
  "And your hair has become very white;
And yet you incessantly stand on your head –
  Do you think, at your age, it is right?"

"In my youth," Father William replied to his son,
  "I feared it might injure the brain;
But, now that I'm perfectly sure I have none,
  Why, I do it again and again."

"You are old," said the youth, "as I mentioned before,
  And you have grown most uncommonly fat;
Yet you turned a back-somersault in at the door –
  Pray, what is the reason of that?"

"In my youth," said the sage, as he shook his grey
 locks,
"I kept all my limbs very supple
By the use of this ointment – one shilling the box –
Allow me to sell you a couple?"

"You are old," said the youth, "and your jaws are too
 weak
For anything tougher than suet;
Yet you finished the goose, with the bones and the
 beak –
Pray, how did you manage to do it?"

"In my youth," said his father, "I took to the law,
And argued each case with my wife;
And the muscular strength, which it gave to my jaw,
Has lasted the rest of my life."

"You are old," said the youth, "one would hardly
 suppose
That your eye was as steady as ever;
Yet you balance an eel on the end of your nose –
What made you so awfully clever?"

"I have answered three questions, and that is enough,"
Said his father; "don't give yourself airs!
Do you think I can listen all day to such stuff?
Be off, or I'll kick you downstairs!"

LEWIS CARROLL

173 **A Nightmare** (From *Iolanthe*)

When you're lying awake with a dismal headache, and
  repose is taboo'd by anxiety,
I conceive you may use any language you choose to
  indulge in without impropriety;
For your brain is on fire – the bedclothes conspire of
  usual slumber to plunder you:
First your counterpane goes and uncovers your toes,
  and your sheet slips demurely from under you;
Then the blanketing tickles – you feel like mixed
  pickles, so terribly sharp is the pricking,
And you're hot, and you're cross, and you tumble and
  toss till there's nothing 'twixt you and the ticking.
Then the bedclothes all creep to the ground in a heap,
  and you pick 'em all up in a tangle;

Next your pillow resigns and politely declines to
  remain at its usual angle!
Well, you get some repose in the form of a doze, with
  hot eye-balls and head ever aching,
But your slumbering teems with such horrible dreams
  that you'd very much better be waking;
For you dream you are crossing the Channel, and
  tossing about in a steamer from Harwich –
Which is something between a large bathing machine
  and a very small second-class carriage –
And you're giving a treat (penny ice and cold meat)
  to a party of friends and relations –
They're a ravenous horde – and they all came on board
  at Sloane Square and South Kensington Stations.
And bound on that journey you find your attorney
  (who started that morning from Devon);
He's a bit undersized, and you don't feel surprised when
  he tells you he's only eleven.
Well, you're driving like mad with this singular lad
  (by the by, the ship's now a four-wheeler),
And you're playing round games, and he calls you bad
  names when you tell him that "ties pay the dealer";
But this you can't stand, so you throw up your hand,
  and you find you're as cold as an icicle,
In your shirt and your socks (the black silk with gold
  clocks), crossing Salisbury Plain on a bicycle:
And he and the crew are on bicycles too – which
  they've somehow or other invested in –
And he's telling the tars all the particulars of a company
  he's interested in –
It's a scheme of devices, to get at low prices all goods
  from cough mixtures to cables

(Which tickled the sailors), by treating retailers as
  though they were all vege*ta*bles –
You get a good spadesman to plant a small tradesman
  (first take off his boots with a boot-tree),
And his legs will take root, and his fingers will shoot,
  and they'll blossom and bud like a fruit-tree –
From the greengrocer tree you get grapes and green
  pea, cauliflower, pineapple and cranberries,
While the pastrycook plant cherry brandy will grant,
  apple puffs, and three-corners, and Banburys –
The shares are a penny, and ever so many are taken by
  Rothschild and Baring,
And just as a few are allotted to you, you awake with
  a shudder despairing –
You're a regular wreck, with a crick in your neck,
  and no wonder you snore, for your head's on the
  floor, and you've needles and pins from your soles
  to your shins, and your flesh is a-creep, for your left
  leg's asleep, and you've cramp in your toes, and a
  fly on your nose, and some fluff in your lung, and a
  feverish tongue, and a thirst that's intense, and a
  general sense that you haven't been sleeping in clover;
But the darkness has passed, and it's daylight at last,
  and the night has been long – ditto ditto my song –
  and thank goodness they're both of them over!

W. S. GILBERT

174 What's the Use?

To a girl who wears trousers

Sure, deck your lower limbs in pants;
Yours are the limbs, my sweeting.
You look divine as you advance –
Have you seen yourself retreating?

OGDEN NASH

175 On a Painted Woman

To youths, who hurry thus away,
  How silly your desire is
At such an early hour to pay
  Your compliments to Iris.

Stop, prithee, stop, ye hasty beaux,
  No longer urge this race on;
Though Iris has put on her clothes,
  She has not put her face on.

PERCY BYSSHE SHELLEY

176 Wise Nature

How wisely Nature, ordering all below,
Forbade on woman's face the hair to grow.
For how could she be shaved, whate'er the barber's
  skill,
Whose tongue would never let her chin be still?

ANONYMOUS

177 **Limericks**

There was a young lady of Riga
Who went for a ride on a tiger;
  They returned from the ride
  With the lady inside,
And a smile on the face of the tiger.

There was an old person of Fratton
Who would go to church with his hat on,
  "If I wake up," he said,
  "With my hat on my head,
I shall know that it hasn't been sat on."

An epicure, dining at Crewe,
Found a large mouse in his stew.
  Said the waiter, "Don't shout
  And wave it about,
Or the rest will be wanting one, too!"

A wonderful bird is the pelican,
His mouth can hold more than his belican.
  He can take in his beak
  Enough food for a week.
I'm darned if I know how the helican!

There was a young lady of Ryde
Who ate some green apples and died.
  The apples fermented
  Inside the lamented,
And made cider inside her inside.

There was a young lady of Bicester,
Who cried out when anyone kissed her,
  But a fellow named Ray
  Caught her out in this way.
He pretended, but then only missed her.

There was a young lady named Bright
Who travelled much faster than light.
  She started one day
  In the relative way
And returned on the previous night.

There was an old fellow of Tring
Who, when somebody asked him to sing,
  Replied, "Ain't it odd?
  I can never tell *God*
Save the Weasel from *Pop goes the King*."

There was a young man of Japan
Whose limericks never would scan;
  When asked why this was,
  He said, "It's because
I always try to get as many words into the last line as
    I possibly can."

ANONYMOUS

178 **The Disagreeable Man**

(From *Princess Ida*)

If you give me your attention, I will tell you what I am:
I'm a genuine philanthropist – all other kinds are sham.
Each little fault of temper and each social defect
In my erring fellow-creatures, I endeavour to correct.
To all their little weaknesses I open people's eyes,
And little plans to snub the self-sufficient I devise;
I love my fellow-creatures – I do all the good I can –
Yet everybody says I'm such a disagreeable man!
  And I can't think why!

To compliments inflated I've a withering reply,
And vanity I always do my best to mortify;
A charitable action I can skilfully dissect;
And interested motives I'm delighted to detect.
I know everybody's income and what everybody earns,
And I carefully compare it with the income-tax returns;
But to benefit humanity, however much I plan,
Yet everybody says I'm such a disagreeable man!
  And I can't think why!

I'm sure I'm no ascetic; I'm as pleasant as can be;
You'll always find me ready with a crushing repartee;
I've an irritating chuckle, I've a celebrated sneer,
I've an entertaining snigger, I've a fascinating leer;
To everybody's prejudice I know a thing or two;
I can tell a woman's age in half a minute – and I do –
But although I try to make myself as pleasant as I can,
Yet everybody says I'm such a disagreeable man!
  And I can't think why!

W. S. GILBERT

179 The Vicar of Bray

In good King Charles's golden days,
  When loyalty no harm meant;
A furious high-church man I was,
  And so I gained preferment.
Unto my flock I daily preached,
  Kings are by God appointed,
And damned are those who dare resist,
  Or touch the Lord's anointed.
  And this is law, I will maintain
      Unto my dying day, Sir,
    That whatsoever King shall reign,
      I will be the Vicar of Bray, Sir!

When Royal James possessed the crown,
  And popery grew in fashion;
The penal law I shouted down,
  And read the declaration:
And I had been a Jesuit,
  But for the Revolution.
    And this is law, I will maintain
      Unto my dying day, Sir,
    That whatsoever King shall reign,
      I will be the Vicar of Bray, Sir!

When William our deliverer came,
  To heal the nation's grievance,
I turned the cat in pan again,
  And swore to him allegiance:
Old principles I did revoke,
  Set conscience at a distance,

Passive obedience is a joke,
  A jest is non-resistance.
    And this is law, I will maintain
      Unto my dying day, Sir,
    That whatsoever King shall reign,
      I will be the Vicar of Bray, Sir!

When glorious Anne became our Queen,
  The Church of England's glory,
Another face of things was seen,
  And I became a Tory:
Occasional conformists base
  I damned, and moderation,
And thought the church in danger was,
  From such prevarication.
    And this is law, I will maintain
      Unto my dying day, Sir,
    That whatsoever King shall reign,
      I will be the Vicar of Bray, Sir!

When George in pudding time came o'er,
  And moderate men looked big, Sir,
My principles I changed once more,
  And so became a Whig, Sir:
And thus preferment I procured,
  From our Faith's Great Defender,
And almost every day abjured
  The Pope, and the Pretender.
    And this is law, I will maintain
      Unto my dying day, Sir,
    That whatsoever King shall reign,
      I will be the Vicar of Bray, Sir!

The illustrious House of Hanover,
  And Protestant succession,
To these I lustily will swear,
  Whilst they can keep possession:
For in my faith, and loyalty,
  I never once will falter,
But George my lawful King shall be,
  Except the times should alter.
    And this is law, I will maintain
      Unto my dying day, Sir,
    That whatsoever King shall reign,
      I will be the Vicar of Bray, Sir!

ANONYMOUS

180 The Irish Pig

'Twas an evening in November,
As I very well remember,
I was strolling down the street in drunken pride,
But my knees were all aflutter,
So I landed in the gutter,
And a pig came up and lay down by my side.

Yes, I lay there in the gutter
Thinking thoughts I could not utter,
When a colleen passing by did softly say,
"You can tell a man that boozes
By the company he chooses."
At that the pig got up and walked away!

ANONYMOUS

181 The Modern Hiawatha

When he killed the Mudjokivis,
Of the skin he made him mittens,
Made them with the fur side inside,
Made them with the skin side outside,
He, to get the warm side inside,
Put the inside skin side outside;
He, to get the cold side outside,
Put the warm side fur side inside.
That's why he put fur side inside,
Why he put the skin side outside,
Why he turned them inside outside.

ANONYMOUS

182 Epitaph for Mike O'Day

This is the grave of Mike O' Day
Who died maintaining his right of way.
His right was clear, his will was strong,
But he's just as dead as if he'd been wrong.

ANONYMOUS

183 Weather Forecast

The rain it raineth every day,
  Upon the just and unjust fellow,
But more upon the just, because
  The unjust has the just's umbrella.

ANONYMOUS

184 The Common Cormorant

The common cormorant or shag
Lays eggs inside a paper bag,
The reason you will see, no doubt,
It is to keep the lightning out.
But what these unobservant birds
Have never noticed is that herds
Of wandering bears may come with buns
And steal the bags to hold the crumbs.

ANONYMOUS

185 The Jester's Song

(From *The Yeomen of the Guard*)

I've wisdom from the East and from the West,
That's subject to no academic rule;
You may find it in the jeering of a jest,
Or distil it from the folly of a fool.
I can teach you with a quip, if I've a mind;
I can trick you into learning with a laugh;
Oh, winnow all my folly, and you'll find
A grain or two of truth among the chaff!

I can set a braggart quailing with a quip,
The upstart I can wither with a whim;
He may wear a merry laugh upon his lip,
But his laughter has an echo that is grim!
When they're offered to the world in merry guise,
Unpleasant truths are swallowed with a will –
For he who'd make his fellow-creatures wise
Should always gild the philosophic pill!

W. S. GILBERT

Poetry is the spontaneous overflow of powerful feelings.
William Wordsworth

186 I Love All Beauteous Things

I love all beauteous things,
  I seek and adore them;
God hath no better praise,
And man in his hasty days
  Is honoured for them.

I too will something make
  And joy in the making;
Although to-morrow it seem
Like the empty words of a dream
  Remembered on waking.

ROBERT BRIDGES

187 **Miracles**

As to me I know of nothing else but miracles,
Whether I walk the streets of Manhattan,
Or dart my sight over the roofs of houses toward the
sky,
Or wade with naked feet along the beach just in the
edge of the water,
Or stand under trees in the woods,
Or talk by day with any one I love,
Or sit at table at dinner with the rest,
Or look at strangers opposite me riding in the car,
Or watch honey bees busy around the hive of a summer
forenoon,
Or animals feeding in the fields,
Or birds, or the wonderfulness of insects in the air,
Or the wonderfulness of the sundown, or of stars
shining so quiet and bright,
Or the exquisite delicate thin curve of the new moon
in spring;
These with the rest, one and all, are to me miracles.

WALT WHITMAN

188 **Music**

When music sounds, gone is the earth I know,
And all her lovely things even lovelier grow;
Her flowers in vision flame, her forest trees
Lift burdened branches, stilled with ecstasies.

When music sounds, out of the water rise
Naiads whose beauty dims my waking eyes,
Rapt in strange dream burns each enchanted face,
With solemn echoing stirs their dwelling-place.

When music sounds, all that I was I am
Ere to this haunt of brooding dust I came;
While from Time's woods break into distant song
The swift-winged hours, as I hasten along.

WALTER DE LA MARE

189 The Fiddler of Dooney

When I play on my fiddle in Dooney,
Folk dance like a wave of the sea;
My cousin is priest in Kilvarnet,
My brother in Moharabuiee.

I passed my brother and cousin:
They read in their books of prayer;
I read in my book of songs
I bought at the Sligo fair.

When we come at the end of time,
To Peter sitting in state,
He will smile on the three old spirits,
But call me first through the gate;

For the good are always the merry,
Save by an evil chance,
And the merry love the fiddle,
And the merry love to dance.

And when the folk there spy me,
They will all come up to me,
With "Here is the fiddler of Dooney!"
And dance like a wave of the sea.

W. B. YEATS

190 Tarantella

Do you remember an Inn,
Miranda?
Do you remember an Inn?
And the tedding and the spreading
Of the straw for a bedding,
And the fleas that tease in the High Pyrenees,
And the wine that tasted of the tar?
And the cheers and the jeers of the young muleteers
(Under the dark of the vine verandah)?
Do you remember an Inn, Miranda,
Do you remember an Inn?
And the cheers and the jeers of the young muleteers
Who hadn't got a penny,
And who weren't paying any,

And the hammer at the doors and the Din?
And the Hip! Hop! Hap!
Of the clap
Of the hands to the twirl and the swirl
Of the girls gone chancing,
Glancing,
Dancing,
Backing and advancing,
Snapping of the clapper to the spin
Out and in –
And the Ting, Tong, Tang of the guitar!
Do you remember an Inn,
Miranda?
Do you remember an Inn?

Never more;
Miranda,
Never more.
Only the high peaks hoar:
And the Aragon a torrent at the door.

No sound
In the walls of the Halls where falls
The tread
Of the feet of the dead to the ground.
No sound:
Only the boom
Of the Waterfall like Doom.

HILAIRE BELLOC

191 **On First Looking into Chapman's Homer**

Much have I travelled in the realms of gold,
And many goodly states and kingdoms seen;
Round many western islands have I been
Which bards in fealty to Apollo hold.
Oft of one wide expanse had I been told
That deep-browed Homer ruled as his demesne:
Yet did I never breathe its pure serene
Till I heard Chapman speak out loud and bold:
Then felt I like some watcher of the skies
When a new planet swims into his ken;
Or like stout Cortez, when with eagle eyes
He stared at the Pacific – and all his men
Looked at each other with a wild surmise –
Silent, upon a peak in Darien.

JOHN KEATS

192 **The Poet** (From *A Midsummer Night's Dream*)

The lunatic, the lover and the poet
Are of imagination all compact: –
One sees more devils than vast hell can hold,
That is, the madman: the lover, all as frantic,
Sees Helen's beauty in a brow of Egypt:
The poet's eye, in a fine frenzy rolling,
Doth glance from heaven to earth, from earth to
  heaven;
And, as imagination bodies forth
The forms of things unknown, the poet's pen
Turns them to shapes, and gives to airy nothing
A local habitation and a name.

WILLIAM SHAKESPEARE

193 Ode

We are the music-makers,
  And we are the dreamers of dreams,
Wandering by lone sea-breakers,
  And sitting by desolate streams;
World-losers and world-forsakers,
  On whom the pale moon gleams:
Yet we are the movers and shakers
  Of the world for ever, it seems.

With wonderful deathless ditties
We build up the world's great cities,
  And out of a fabulous story
  We fashion an empire's glory;
One man with a dream, at pleasure,
  Shall go forth and conquer a crown;
And three with a new song's measure
  Can trample an empire down.

We, in the ages lying
  In the buried past of the earth,
Built Nineveh with our sighing,
  And Babel itself with our mirth;
And o'erthrew them with prophesying
  To the old of the new world's worth;
For each age is a dream that is dying,
  Or one that is coming to birth.

A. W. O'SHAUGHNESSY

194 **Orpheus with His Lute**

(From *Henry VIII*)

Orpheus with his lute made trees
And the mountain-tops that freeze
  Bow themselves when he did sing:
To his music plants and flowers
Ever sprung; as sun and showers
  There had made a lasting spring.

Every thing that heard him play,
Even the billows of the sea,
  Hung their heads and then lay by.
In sweet music is such art,
Killing care and grief of heart
  Fall asleep, or hearing, die.

WILLIAM SHAKESPEARE

195 **Words**

Out of us all
That make rhymes,
Will you choose
Sometimes –
As the winds use
A crack in a wall
Or a drain,
Their joy or their pain
To whistle through –
Choose me,
You English words?

I know you:
You are light as dreams,
Tough as oak,
Precious as gold,
As poppies and corn,
Or an old cloak;
Sweet as our birds
To the ear,
As the burnet rose
In the heat
Of Midsummer.
Strange as the races
Of dead and unborn:
Strange and sweet
Equally,
And familiar,
To the eye,
As the dearest faces

That a man knows,
And as lost homes are:
But though older far
Than oldest yew, –
As our hills are, old, –
Worn new
Again and again:
Young as our streams
After rain:
And as dear
As the earth which you prove
That we love.

Make me content
With some sweetness
From Wales,
Whose nightingales
Have no wings, –
From Wiltshire and Kent
And Herefordshire,
And all the villages there, –
From the names, and the things
No less.
Let me sometimes dance
With you,
Or climb,
Or stand perchance
In ecstasy,
Fixed and free
In a rhyme,
As poets do.

EDWARD THOMAS

196 On the Grasshopper and Cricket

The poetry of earth is never dead:
  When all the birds are faint with the hot sun,
  And hide in cooling trees, a voice will run
From hedge to hedge about the new-mown mead;
That is the Grasshopper's – he takes the lead
  In summer luxury, – he has never done
  With his delights; for when tired out with fun
He rests at ease beneath some pleasant weed.
The poetry of earth is ceasing never:
  On a lone winter evening, when the frost
    Has wrought a silence, from the stove there shrills
The Cricket's song, in warmth increasing ever,
  And seems to one in drowsiness half lost,
    The Grasshopper's among some grassy hills.

JOHN KEATS

197 **Westminster Bridge**

Earth has not anything to show more fair:
Dull would he be of soul who could pass by
A sight so touching in its majesty:
This City now doth, like a garment, wear
The beauty of the morning; silent, bare,
Ships, towers, domes, theatres, and temples lie
Open unto the fields, and to the sky;
All bright and glittering in the smokeless air.
Never did sun more beautifully steep
In his first splendour, valley, rock, or hill,
Ne'er saw I, never felt, a calm so deep!
The river glideth at his own sweet will:
Dear God! the very houses seem asleep;
And all that mighty heart is lying still!

WILLIAM WORDSWORTH

198 London

Athwart the sky a lowly sigh
  From west to east the sweet wind carried;
The sun stood still on Primrose Hill;
  His light in all the city tarried:
The clouds on viewless columns bloomed
Like smouldering lilies unconsumed.

"Oh sweetheart, see! how shadowy,
  Of some occult magician's rearing,
Or swung in space of heaven's grace
  Dissolving, dimly reappearing,
Afloat upon ethereal tides
St. Paul's above the city rides!"

A rumour broke through the thin smoke
  Enwreathing abbey, tower, and palace,
The parks, the squares, the thoroughfares,
  The million-peopled lanes and alleys,
An ever-muttering prisoned storm,
The heart of London beating warm.

JOHN DAVIDSON

199 **Sunken Evening**

The green light floods the city square –
  A sea of fowl and feathered fish,
  Where squalls of rainbirds dive and splash
And dusty sparrows chop the air.

Submerged, the prawn-blue pigeons feed
  In sandy grottoes round the Mall,
  And crusted lobster-buses crawl
Among the fountains' silver weed.

There, like a wreck, with mast and bell,
  The torn church settles by the bow,
  While phosphorescent starlings stow
Their mussel shells along the hull.

The oyster-poet, drowned but dry,
  Rolls a black pearl between his bones;
  The mermaid, trapped by telephones,
Gazes in bubbles at the sky.

Till, with the dark, the shallows run,
  And homeward surges tide and fret –
  The slow night trawls its heavy net
And hauls the clerk to Surbiton.

LAURIE LEE

200 **Within King's College Chapel, Cambridge**

Tax not the royal Saint with vain expense,
With ill-matched aims the Architect who planned –
Albeit labouring for a scanty band
Of white-robed Scholars only – this immense
And glorious work of fine intelligence!
Give all thou canst; high Heaven rejects the lore
Of nicely-calculated less or more;
So deemed the man who fashioned for the sense
These lofty pillars, spread that branching roof
Self-poised, and scooped into ten thousand cells,
Where light and shade repose, where music dwells
Lingering – and wandering on as loth to die;
Like thoughts whose very sweetness yieldeth proof
That they were born for immortality.

WILLIAM WORDSWORTH

201 **King's College Chapel**

When to the music of Byrd or Tallis,
  The ruffed boys singing in the blackened stalls,
The candles lighting the small bones on their faces,
  The Tudors stiff in marble on the walls,

There comes to evensong Elizabeth or Henry,
  Rich with brocade, pearl, golden lilies, at the altar,
The scarlet lions leaping on their bosoms,
  Pale royal hands fingering the crackling psalter,

Henry is thinking of his lute and of backgammon,
  Elizabeth follows the waving song, the mystery,
Proud in her red wig and green jewelled favours;
  They sit in their white lawn sleeves, as cool as history.

CHARLES CAUSLEY

202 **Fare Well**

When I lie where shades of darkness
Shall no more assail mine eyes,
Nor the rain make lamentation
  When the wind sighs;
How will fare the world whose wonder
Was the very proof of me?
Memory fades, must the remembered
  Perishing be?

Oh, when this my dust surrenders
Hand, foot, lip, to dust again,
May those loved and loving faces
  Please other men!
May the rusting harvest hedgerow
Still the Traveller's Joy entwine,
And as happy children gather
  Posies once mine.

Look thy last on all things lovely,
Every hour. Let no night
Seal thy sense in deathly slumber
  Till to delight
Thou have paid thy utmost blessing;
Since that all things thou wouldst praise
Beauty took from those who loved them
  In other days.

WALTER DE LA MARE

11 LOVE — ITS JOYS

Poetry is imaginative passion.

Leigh Hunt

203 Love

Love lives beyond
The tomb, the earth, which fades like dew –
I love the fond,
The faithful, and the true.

Love lies in sleep,
'Tis happiness of healthy dreams,
Eve's dews may weep,
But love delightful seems.

'Tis seen in flowers,
And in the even's pearly dew,
On earth's green hours,
And in the heaven's eternal blue.

'Tis heard in spring
When light and sunbeams, warm and kind,
On angel's wing
Bring love and music to the mind.

And where's the voice,
So young, so beautiful, and sweet
As nature's choice,
Where spring and lovers meet?

Love lives beyond
The tomb, the earth, the flowers, and dew.
I love the fond,
The faithful, young, and true.

JOHN CLARE

204 The Power of Love

(From *A Midsummer Night's Dream*)

Things base and vile, holding no quantity,
Love can transpose to form and dignity.
Love looks not with the eyes, but with the mind,
And therefore is winged Cupid painted blind.
Nor hath Love's mind of any judgement taste;
Wings, and no eyes, figure unheedy haste.
And therefore is Love said to be a child,
Because in choice he is so oft beguiled.
As waggish boys in game themselves forswear,
So the boy Love is perjured everywhere.

WILLIAM SHAKESPEARE

205 The Power of Words

(From *Two Gentlemen of Verona*)

Say that upon the altar of her beauty
You sacrifice your tears, your sighs, your heart;
Write till your ink be dry, and with your tears
Moist it again, and frame some feeling line
That may discover such integrity;
For Orpheus' lute was strung with poets' sinews;
Whose golden touch could soften steel and stones,
Make tigers tame, and huge leviathans
Forsake unsounded deeps to dance on sands.

WILLIAM SHAKESPEARE

206 Fain Would I Change That Note

Fain would I change that note
  To which fond love hath charmed me
Long, long to sing by rote,
  Fancying that that harmed me.
Yet when this thought doth come,
"Love is the perfect sum
  Of all delight,"
I have no other choice
Either for pen or voice
  To sing or write.

O love! they wrong thee much
  That say thy sweet is bitter,
When thy ripe fruit is such
  As nothing can be sweeter.
Fair house of joy and bliss
Where truest pleasure is,
  I do adore thee:
I know thee what thou art,
I serve thee with my heart
  And fall before thee.

ANONYMOUS

207 The Triple Fool

I am two fools, I know,
For loving, and for saying so
In whining poetry;
But where's that wise man, that would not be I,
If she would not deny?
Then as the earth's inward narrow crooked lanes
Do purge sea-water's fretful salt away,
I thought, if I could draw my pains,
Through rhyme's vexation, I should them allay.
Grief brought to numbers cannot be so fierce,
For he tames it, that fetters it in verse.

But when I have done so,
Some man, his art and voice to show,
Doth set and sing my pain,
And, by delighting many, frees again
Grief, which verse did restrain.
To love and grief tribute of verse belongs,
But not of such as pleases when 'tis read;
Both are increasèd by such songs:
For both their triumphs so are publishèd,
And I, which was two fools, do so grow three;
Who are a little wise, the best fools be.

JOHN DONNE

208 There Is a Lady Sweet and Kind

There is a lady sweet and kind,
Was never face so pleased my mind;
I did but see her passing by,
And yet I love her till I die.

Her gesture, motion, and her smiles
Her wit, her voice my heart beguiles,
Beguiles my heart, I know not why,
And yet I love her till I die.

Her free behaviour, winning looks,
Will make a lawyer burn his books;
I touched her not, alas! not I,
And yet I love her till I die.

Had I her fast betwixt mine arms,
Judge you that think such sports were harms;
Weren't any harm? no, no, fie, fie,
For I will love her till I die.

Should I remain confinèd there
So long as Phoebus in his sphere,
I to request, she to deny,
Yet would I love her till I die.

Cupid is winged and doth range,
Her country so my love doth change:
But change she earth, or change she sky,
Yet will I love her till I die.

ANONYMOUS

209 Song

How sweet I roamed from field to field
And tasted all the summer's pride,
'Till I the prince of love beheld
Who in the sunny beams did glide.

He showed me lilies for my hair,
And blushing roses for my brow;
He led me through his gardens fair
Where all his golden pleasures grow.

With sweet May-dews my wings were wet,
And Phoebus fired my vocal rage;
He caught me in his silken net,
And shut me in his golden cage.

He loves to sit and hear me sing,
Then, laughing, sports and plays with me;
Then stretches out my golden wing,
And mocks my loss of liberty.

WILLIAM BLAKE

210 Triolet

When first we met we did not guess
That Love would prove so hard a master;
Of more than common friendliness
When first we met we did not guess.
Who could foretell this sore distress,
This irretrievable disaster
When first we met? – We did not guess
That Love would prove so hard a master.

ROBERT BRIDGES

211 To His Love

Music, when soft voices die,
Vibrates in the memory –
Odours, when sweet violets sicken,
Live within the sense they quicken.

Rose leaves, when the rose is dead,
Are heaped for the belovèd's bed;
And so my thoughts, when thou art gone,
Love itself shall slumber on.

PERCY BYSSHE SHELLEY

212 Out Upon It!

Out upon it! I have loved
  Three whole days together;
And am like to love three more,
  If it prove fair weather.

Time shall moult away his wings,
  Ere he shall discover
In the whole wide world again
  Such a constant lover.

But the spite on't is, no praise
  Is due at all to me:
Love with me had made no stays,
  Had it any been but she.

Had it any been but she,
  And that very face,
There had been at least ere this
  A dozen dozen in her place.

JOHN SUCKLING

213 Love Me Not for Comely Grace

Love me not for comely grace,
For my pleasing eye or face,
Nor for any outward part,
No, nor for my constant heart,
  For those may fail or turn to ill,
    So thou and I shall sever:
Keep therefore a true woman's eye,
And love me still, but know not why,
  So hast thou the same reason still
    To dote upon me ever.

ANONYMOUS

214 If Thou Must Love Me

If thou must love me, let it be for nought
  Except for love's sake only. Do not say,
  "I love her for her smile – her look – her way
Of speaking gently, – for a trick of thought
That falls in well with mine, and certes brought
  A sense of pleasant ease on such a day" –
  For these things in themselves, Belovèd, may
Be changed, or change for thee – and love, so wrought,
May be unwrought so. Neither love me for
  Thine own dear pity's wiping my cheeks dry:
A creature might forget to weep, who bore
  Thy comfort long, and lose thy love thereby!
But love me for love's sake, that evermore
  Thou may'st love on, through love's eternity.

ELIZABETH BARRETT BROWNING

215 **Love's Philosophy**

The fountains mingle with the river
  And the rivers with the ocean,
The winds of heaven mix for ever
  With a sweet emotion;
Nothing in the world is single,
  All things by a law divine
In one another's being mingle –
  Why not I with thine?

See the mountains kiss high heaven
  And the waves clasp one another;
No sister-flower would be forgiven
  If it disdained its brother:
And the sunlight clasps the earth,
  And the moonbeams kiss the sea –
What are all these kissings worth,
  If thou kiss not me?

PERCY BYSSHE SHELLEY

216 Sonnet

Let me not to the marriage of true minds
Admit impediments. Love is not love
Which alters when it alteration finds,
Or bends with the remover to remove.
O no! it is an ever-fixèd mark,
That looks on tempests and is never shaken;
It is the star to every wandering bark,
Whose worth's unknown, although his height be taken.
Love's not Time's fool, though rosy lips and cheeks
Within his bending sickle's compass come;
Love alters not with his brief hours and weeks,
But bears it out even to the edge of doom.
  If this be error, and upon me proved,
  I never writ, nor no man ever loved.

WILLIAM SHAKESPEARE

217 Dear, if You Change

Dear, if you change, I'll never choose again.
Sweet, if you shrink, I'll never think of love.
Fair, if you fail, I'll judge all beauty vain.
Wise, if too weak, my wits I'll never prove.
  Dear, sweet, fair, wise, change, shrink, nor be not weak:
  And, on my faith, my faith shall never break.

Earth with her flowers shall sooner heaven adorn,
Heaven her bright stars through earth's dim globe shall move,
Fire heat shall lose, and forests of flame be borne,
Air made to shine as black as hell shall prove:
  Earth, heaven, fire, air, the world transformed shall view,
  Ere I prove false to faith, or strange to you.

ANONYMOUS

218 My True Love Hath My Heart

My true love hath my heart, and I have his,
  By just exchange one for another given;
I hold his dear, and mine he cannot miss,
  There never was a better bargain driven:
    My true love hath my heart and I have his.

His heart in me keeps him and me in one,
  My heart in him his thoughts and senses guides;
He loves my heart, for once it was his own,
  I cherish his, because in me it bides:
    My true love hath my heart, and I have his.

PHILIP SIDNEY

219 **The Scrutiny**

Why should I swear I am forsworn,
  Since thine I vowed to be?
Lady it is already morn,
  And 'twas last night I swore to thee
That fond impossibility.

Have I not loved thee much and long,
  A tedious twelve hours' space?
I must all other beauties wrong,
  And rob thee of a new embrace;
Could I still dote upon thy face.

Not, but all joy in thy brown hair,
  By others may be found;
But I must search the black and fair
  Like skilful mineralists that sound
For treasure in unploughed-up ground.

Then, if when I have loved my round,
  Thou prov'st the pleasant she;
With spoils of meaner beauties crowned,
  I laden will return to thee,
Even sated with variety.

RICHARD LOVELACE

220 The Girl's Confession

He loves me for imagined excellences
I never owned or claimed:
Not least for my body, whose upkeep is costly
And whose movements are others', carefully mimed.

He is unaware of the irony,
As he was of the preparation, the endless preening;
The hours before the mirror; the slow walk
With books on head, the expensive course in grooming.

He has bought books for me, afterwards praising
My book-taught erudition;
His refusal to face my fact makes me sacrosanct,
Would make him describe as modesty this confession.

Yet the view from this pedestal is pleasantly heady;
And perhaps, such is my elevation, he need never see
The imperfections which I certainly share
With the old loves, unloved now, who went before
me.

Thus may I give to him the one great excellence
I have: my love for him, which alone he fails to praise.
If so, so be it. Let there be this sweet
Misunderstanding to the end of our shared days,

For above all am I glad to be his chosen,
And to be loved, albeit for the wrong reason.

ERIC MILLWARD

221 Break of Day

Stay, O sweet, and do not rise!
The light that shines comes from thine eyes;
The day breaks not: it is my heart,
Because that you and I must part.
Stay! or else my joys will die
And perish in their infancy.

JOHN DONNE ?

222 How Do I Love Thee?

How do I love thee? Let me count the ways.
I love thee to the depth and breadth and height
My soul can reach, when feeling out of sight
For the ends of Being and ideal Grace.
I love thee to the level of every day's
Most quiet need, by sun and candlelight.
I love thee freely, as men strive for Right;
I love thee purely, as they turn from Praise.
I love thee with the passion put to use
In my old griefs, and with my childhood's faith.
I love thee with a love I seemed to lose
With my lost saints, – I love thee with the breath,
Smiles, tears, of all my life! – and, if God choose,
I shall but love thee better after death.

ELIZABETH BARRETT BROWNING

223 **The Album**

I see you, a child
In a garden sheltered for buds and playtime,
Listening as if beguiled
By a fancy beyond your years and the flowering
  maytime.
The print is faded: soon there will be
No trace of that pose enthralling,
Nor visible echo of my voice distantly calling
"Wait! Wait for me!"

Then I turn the page
To a girl who stands like a questioning iris
By the waterside, at an age
That asks every mirror to tell what the heart's desire is.
The answer she finds in that oracle stream
Only time could affirm or disprove,
Yet I wish I was there to venture a warning, "Love
Is not what you dream."

Next you appear
As if garlands of wild felicity crowned you –
Courted, caressed, you wear
Like immortelles the lovers and friends around you.
"They will not last you, rain or shine,
They are but straws and shadows,"
I cry: "Give not to those charming desperadoes
What was made to be mine."

One picture is missing –
The last. It would show me a tree stripped bare
By intemperate gales, her amazing
Noonday of blossom spoilt which promised so fair.
Yet, scanning those scenes at your heyday taken,
I tremble, as one who must view
In the crystal a doom he could never deflect – yes, I too
Am fruitlessly shaken.

I close the book;
But the past slides out of its leaves to haunt me
And it seems, wherever I look,
Phantoms of irreclaimable happiness taunt me.
Then I see her petalled, in new-blown hours,
Beside me – "All you love most there
Has blossomed again," she murmurs, "all that you
missed there
Has grown to be yours."

C. DAY LEWIS

224 **Meeting at Night**

The grey sea and the long black land;
And the yellow half-moon large and low;
And the startled little waves that leap
In fiery ringlets from their sleep,
As I gain the cove with pushing prow,
And quench its speed i' the slushy sand.

Then a mile of warm sea-scented beach;
Three fields to cross till a farm appears;
A tap at the pane, the quick sharp scratch
And blue spurt of a lighted match,
And a voice less loud, through its joys and fears,
Than the two hearts beating each to each!

ROBERT BROWNING

225 **The Visitation**

Drowsing in my chair of disbelief
I watch the door as it slowly opens –
A trick of the night wind?

Your slender body seems a shaft of moonlight
Against the door as it gently closes.
Do you cast no shadow?

Your whisper is too soft for credence,
Your tread like blossom drifting from a bough,
Your touch even softer.

You wear that sorrowful and tender mask
Which on high mountain tops in heather-flow
Entrances lonely shepherds;

And though a single word scatters all doubts
I quake for wonder at your choice of me:
Why, why and why?

ROBERT GRAVES

226 Letter from Town: The Almond-Tree

You promised to send me some violets. Did you
forget?
White ones and blue ones from under the orchard
hedge?
Sweet dark purple, and white ones mixed for a
pledge
Of our early love that hardly has opened yet.

Here there's an almond-tree – you have never seen
Such a one in the north – it flowers on the street,
and I stand
Every day by the fence to look up at the flowers
that expand
At rest in the blue, and wonder at what they mean.

Under the almond-tree, the happy lands
Provence, Japan, and Italy repose;
And passing feet are chatter and clapping of those
Who play around us, country girls clapping their
hands.

You, my love, the foremost, in a flowered gown,
All your unbearable tenderness, you with the laughter
Startled upon your eyes now so wide with
hereafter,
You with loose hands of abandonment hanging down.

D. H. LAWRENCE

227 The Cloths of Heaven

Had I the heavens' embroidered cloths,
Enwrought with golden and silver light,
The blue and the dim and the dark cloths
Of night and light and the half light,
I would spread the cloths under your feet:
But I, being poor, have only my dreams;
I have spread my dreams under your feet;
Tread softly because you tread on my dreams.

W. B. YEATS

228 The Turtle-Dove

O don't you see the turtle-dove
  Sitting under yonder tree
Lamenting for her own true love?
  And I will mourn for thee, my dear,
  And I will mourn for thee.

If you must suffer grief and pain,
  'Tis but for a little while;
For, though I go away, I'll return again,
  If I row ten thousand mile, my dear,
  If I row ten thousand mile!

Ten thousand mile is very far
  For me to bide alone
With a heavy, heavy sigh, and a bitter, bitter cry;
  No one to hear my moan, my dear,
  No one to hear my moan.

I may not stay your grievous moan,
  Your pain I may not ease;
Yet I will love but thee alone;
  Till the streams run from the seas, my dear,
  Till the streams run from the seas!

The tides shall cease to beat the shore,
  The stars fall from the sky;
Yet I will love thee more and more
  Until the day I die, my dear,
  Until the day I die.

Then let the seas run dry, sweetheart,
  The rocks melt in the sun,
Yet here I will stay, nor ever from thee part,
  Till all my days are done, my dear,
  Till all my days are done!

ANONYMOUS

229 Sonnet

Shall I compare thee to a summer's day?
Thou art more lovely and more temperate:
Rough winds do shake the darling buds of May,
And summer's lease hath all too short a date:
Sometime too hot the eye of heaven shines,
And often is his gold complexion dimmed;
And every fair from fair sometime declines,
By chance or nature's changing course untrimmed;
But thy eternal summer shall not fade,
Nor lose possession of that fair thou owest;
Nor shall Death brag thou wanderest in his shade,
When in eternal lines to time thou growest:
  So long as men can breathe, or eyes can see,
  So long lives this, and this gives life to thee.

WILLIAM SHAKESPEARE

230 To Dianeme

Sweet, be not proud of those two eyes,
Which star-like sparkle in their skies;
Nor be you proud that you can see
All hearts your captives; yours, yet free:
Be you not proud of that rich hair
Which wantons with the love-sick air:
Whenas that ruby which you wear,
Sunk from the tip of your soft ear,
Will last to be a precious stone
When all your world of beauty's gone.

ROBERT HERRICK

231 I Will Make You Brooches

I will make you brooches and toys for your delight
Of bird-song at morning and star-shine at night.
I will make a palace fit for you and me
Of green days in forests and blue days at sea.

I will make my kitchen, and you shall keep your room,
Where white flows the river and bright blows the
  broom.
And you shall wash your linen and keep your body
  white
In rainfall at morning and dewfall at night.

And this shall be for music when no one else is near,
The fine song for singing, the rare song to hear!
That only I remember, that only you admire,
Of the broad road that stretches and the roadside fire.

ROBERT LOUIS STEVENSON

232 **To Celia**

Drink to me only with thine eyes,
  And I will pledge with mine;
Or leave a kiss but in the cup
  And I'll not look for wine.
The thirst that from the soul doth rise
  Doth ask a drink divine;
But might I of Jove's nectar sup,
  I would not change for thine.

I sent thee late a rosy wreath,
  Not so much honouring thee
As giving it a hope that there
  It could not withered be;
But thou thereon didst only breathe,
  And sent'st it back to me;
Since when it grows, and smells, I swear,
  Not of itself but thee!

BEN JONSON

233 **A Love Song** (From *Twelfth Night*)

O mistress mine, where are you roaming?
O stay and hear! your true love's coming,
  That can sing both high and low:
Trip no further, pretty sweeting;
Journeys end in lovers' meeting,
  Every wise man's son doth know.

What is love? 'tis not hereafter;
Present mirth hath present laughter;
  What's to come is still unsure:
In delay there lies no plenty;
Then come kiss me, sweet-and-twenty!
Youth's a stuff will not endure.

WILLIAM SHAKESPEARE

234 **She Walks in Beauty**

She walks in beauty, like the night
  Of cloudless climes and starry skies;
And all that's best of dark and bright
  Meet in her aspect and her eyes:
Thus mellowed to that tender light
  Which heaven to gaudy day denies.

One shade the more, one ray the less,
  Had half impaired the nameless grace
Which waves in every raven tress,
  Or softly lightens o'er her face;
Where thoughts serenely sweet express
  How pure, how dear their dwelling-place.

And on that cheek and o'er that brow
  So soft, so calm, yet eloquent,
The smiles that win, the tints that glow
  But tell of days in goodness spent,
A mind at peace with all below,
  A heart whose love is innocent!

GEORGE GORDON BYRON

235 Cherry Ripe

There is a garden in her face,
Where roses and white lilies grow;
A heavenly paradise is that place,
Wherein all pleasant fruits do flow.
There cherries grow which none may buy
Till "Cherry ripe" themselves do cry.

Those cherries fairly do enclose
Of orient pearl a double row,
Which when her lovely laughter shows,
They look like rose-buds filled with snow.
Yet them not peer nor prince can buy,
Till "Cherry ripe" themselves do cry.

Her eyes like angels watch them still;
Her brows like bended bows do stand,
Threatening with piercing frowns to kill
All that attempt with eye or hand
Those sacred cherries to come nigh,
Till "Cherry ripe" themselves do cry.

THOMAS CAMPION

236 **The Arrival of Cleopatra**

(From *Anthony and Cleopatra*)

The barge she sat in, like a burnished throne,
Burnt on the water. The poop was beaten gold,
Purple the sails, and so perfumèd that
The winds were love-sick with them. The oars were
  silver,
Which to the tune of flutes kept stroke, and made
The water which they beat to follow faster,
As amorous of their strokes. For her own person,
It beggared all description; she did lie
In her pavilion – cloth-of-gold of tissue –
O'er-picturing that Venus where we see
The fancy outwork nature. On each side her
Stood pretty dimpled boys, like smiling Cupids,
With divers-coloured fans, whose wind did seem
To glow the delicate cheeks which they did cool,
And what they undid did.

WILLIAM SHAKESPEARE

237 **Who Is Silvia?** (From *Two Gentlemen of Verona*)

Who is Silvia? What is she,
  That all our swains commend her?
Holy, fair, and wise is she,
  The heaven such grace did lend her,
That she might admirèd be.

Is she kind as she is fair?
  For beauty lives with kindness:
Love doth to her eyes repair,
  To help him of his blindness,
And, being helped, inhabits there.

Then to Silvia let us sing,
  That Silvia is excelling;
She excels each mortal thing
  Upon the dull earth dwelling:
To her let us garlands bring.

WILLIAM SHAKESPEARE

238 **Her Triumph**

See the chariot at hand here of love,
   Wherein my lady rideth!
Each that draws is a swan or a dove,
   And well the car love guideth.
As she goes all hearts do duty
                  Unto her beauty;
And enamoured do wish, so they might
                  But enjoy such a sight,
That they still were to run by her side,
Through swords, through seas, whither she would
      ride.

Do but look on her eyes, they do light
  All that love's world compriseth!
Do but look on her hair, it is bright
  As love's star when it riseth!
Do but mark, her forehead's smoother
                    Than words that soothe her;
And from her arched brows such a grace
                    Sheds itself through the face,
As alone there triumphs to the life
All the gain, all the good, of the elements' strife.

Have you seen but a bright lily grow
  Before rude hands have touched it?
Have you marked but the fall of the snow
  Before the soil hath smutched it?
Have you felt the wool of beaver,
                    Or swan's down ever?
Or have smelt o' the bud o' the brier,
                    Or the nard in the fire?
Or have tasted the bag of the bee?
O so white, O so soft, O so sweet is she!

BEN JONSON

239 He That Loves a Rosy Cheek

He that loves a rosy cheek
  Or a coral lip admires,
Or from star-like eyes doth seek
  Fuel to maintain his fires;
As old Time makes these decay,
So his flames must waste away.

But a smooth and steadfast mind,
  Gentle thoughts and calm desires,
Hearts with equal love combined,
  Kindle never-dying fires:
Where these are not, I despise
Lovely cheeks or lips or eyes.

THOMAS CAREW

240 **Dover Beach**

The sea is calm to-night.
The tide is full, the moon lies fair
Upon the straits; – on the French coast the light
Gleams and is gone; the cliffs of England stand,
Glimmering and vast, out in the tranquil bay.
Come to the window, sweet is the night air!
Only, from the long line of spray
Where the sea meets the moon-blanched land,
Listen! you hear the grating roar
Of pebbles which the waves draw back, and fling,
At their return, up the high strand,
Begin, and cease, and then again begin,
With tremulous cadence slow, and bring
The eternal note of sadness in.

Sophocles long ago
Heard it on the Aegean, and it brought
Into his mind the turbid ebb and flow
Of human misery; we
Find also in the sound a thought,
Hearing it by this distant northern sea.

The Sea of Faith
Was once, too, at the full, and round earth's shore
Lay like the folds of a bright girdle furled.
But now I only hear
Its melancholy, long, withdrawing roar,
Retreating, to the breath
Of the night-wind, down the vast edges drear
And naked shingles of the world.

Ah, love, let us be true
To one another! for the world, which seems
To lie before us like a land of dreams,
So various, so beautiful, so new,
Hath really neither joy, nor love, nor light,
Nor certitude, nor peace, nor help for pain;
And we are here as on a darkling plain
Swept with confused alarms of struggle and flight,
Where ignorant armies clash by night.

MATTHEW ARNOLD

We do not understand a great poem till we have felt it through and as far as possible recreated in ourselves the emotions which it originally carried.

Gilbert Murray

241 **Love Is a Sickness**

Love is a sickness full of woes,
  All remedies refusing;
A plant that with most cutting grows,
  Most barren with best using.
          Why so?
More we enjoy it, more it dies;
If not enjoyed, it sighing cries –
          Heigh ho!

Love is a torment of the mind,
  A tempest everlasting;
And Jove hath made it of a kind
  Not well, nor full nor fasting.
          Why so?
More we enjoy it, more it dies;
If not enjoyed, it sighing cries –
          Heigh ho!

SAMUEL DANIEL

242 When You Are Old

When you are old and gray and full of sleep,
And nodding by the fire, take down this book,
And slowly read, and dream of the soft look
Your eyes had once, and of their shadows deep;

How many loved your moments of glad grace,
And loved your beauty with love false or true;
But one man loved the pilgrim soul in you,
And loved the sorrows of your changing face;

And bending down beside the glowing bars,
Murmur, a little sadly, how love fled
And paced upon the mountains overhead,
And hid his face amid a crowd of stars.

W. B. YEATS

243 The Straw

Peace, the wild valley streaked with torrents,
A hoopoe perched on his warm rock. Then why
This tremor of the straw between my fingers?

What should I fear? Have I not testimony
In her own hand, signed with her own name
That my love fell as lightning on her heart?

These questions, bird, are not rhetorical.
Watch how the straw twitches and leaps
As though the earth quaked at a distance.

Requited love; but better unrequited
If this chance instrument gives warning
Of cataclysmic anguish far away.

Were she at ease, warmed by the thoughts of me,
Would not my hand stay steady as this rock?
Have I undone her by my vehemence?

ROBERT GRAVES

244 **By Ferry to the Island**

We crossed by ferry to the bare island
where sheep and cows stared coldly through the wind –
the sea behind us with its silver water,
the silent ferryman standing in the stern
clutching his coat about him like old iron.

We landed from the ferry and went inland
past a small church down to the winding shore
where a white seagull fallen from the failing
chill and ancient daylight lay so pure
and softly breasted that it made more dear

the lesser white around us. There we sat
sheltered by a rock beside the sea.
Someone made coffee, someone played the fool
in a high rising voice for two hours.
The sea's language was more grave and harsh.

And one sat there whose dress was white and cool.
The fool sparkled his wit that she might hear
new diamonds turning on her naked finger.
What might the sea think or the dull sheep
lifting its head through heavy Sunday sleep?

And later, going home, a moon rising
at the end of a cart-track, minimum of red,
the wind being dark, imperfect cows staring
out of their half-intelligence, and a plough
lying on its side in the cold, raw

naked twilight, there began to move
slowly, like heavy water, in the heart
the image of the gull and of that dress,
both being white and out of the darkness rising
the moon ahead of us with its rusty ring.

IAIN CRICHTON SMITH

245 The Shy Lover

I often longed, when wandering up and down,
To hear the rustle of thy Sunday gown;
And when we met, I passed, and let thee go,
And felt I loved, but dare not tell thee so:
Snares are so thickly spread on woman's way,
The common ballad teaches, men betray.
I thought and felt it rudeness if I tried,
And well-meant kindness might be misapplied.
I longed to walk with thee, where waters play
And lined with water-cresses all the way;
And read the poets as I went along
And thought they knew thy name in every song.
The mind on thee and beauty's music dwells,
And listens to the sound of Glinton bells.

JOHN CLARE

246 Down by the Salley Gardens

Down by the salley gardens my love and I did meet;
She passed the salley gardens with little snow-white feet.
She bid me take love easy, as the leaves grow on the tree;
But I, being young and foolish, with her would not agree.

In a field by the river my love and I did stand,
And on my leaning shoulder she laid her snow-white hand.
She bid me take life easy, as the grass grows on the weirs;
But I was young and foolish, and now am full of tears.

W. B. YEATS

247 A Thunderstorm in Town

A reminiscence: 1893

She wore a new "terra-cotta" dress,
And we stayed, because of the pelting storm,
Within the hansom's dry recess,
Though the horse had stopped; yea, motionless
  We sat on, snug and warm.

Then the downpour ceased, to my sharp sad pain
And the glass that had screened our forms before
Flew up, and out she sprang to her door:
I should have kissed her if the rain
  Had lasted a minute more.

THOMAS HARDY

248 **The Passionate Shepherd to His Love**

Come live with me and be my love,
And we will all the pleasures prove
That hills and valleys, dale and field,
And all the craggy mountains yield.

There will we sit upon the rocks,
And see the shepherds feed their flocks
By shallow rivers, to whose falls
Melodious birds sing madrigals.

There will I make thee beds of roses
And a thousand fragrant posies,
A cap of flowers, and a kirtle
Embroidered all with leaves of myrtle.

A gown made of the finest wool,
Which from our pretty lambs we pull,
Fair-linèd slippers for the cold,
With buckles of the purest gold.

A belt of straw and ivy buds
With coral clasps and amber studs:
And if these pleasures may thee move,
Come live with me and be my love.

Thy silver dishes for thy meat
As precious as the gods do eat,
Shall on an ivory table be
Prepared each day for thee and me.

The shepherd swains shall dance and sing
For thy delight each May morning:
If these delights thy mind may move,
Then live with me and be my love.

CHRISTOPHER MARLOWE

249 Come, Live with Me and Be My Love

Come, live with me and be my love,
And we will all the pleasures prove
Of peace and plenty, bed and board,
That chance employment may afford.

I'll handle dainties on the docks
And thou shalt read of summer frocks:
At evening by the sour canals
We'll hope to hear some madrigals.

Care on thy maiden brow shall put
A wreath of wrinkles, and thy foot
Be shod with pain: not silken dress
But toil shall tire thy loveliness.

Hunger shall make thy modest zone
And cheat fond death of all but bone –
If these delights thy mind may move,
Then live with me and be my love.

C. DAY LEWIS

250 The Cap and Bells

The jester walked in the garden:
The garden had fallen still;
He bade his soul rise upward
And stand on her window-sill.

It rose in a straight blue garment,
When owls began to call:
It had grown wise-tongued by thinking
Of a quiet and light footfall;

But the young queen would not listen;
She rose in her pale night-gown;
She drew in her heavy casement
And pushed the latches down.

He bade his heart go to her,
When the owls called out no more;
In a red and quivering garment
It sang to her through the door.

It had grown sweet-tongued by dreaming
Of a flutter of flower-like hair;
But she took up her fan from the table
And waved it off in the air.

"I have cap and bells," he pondered,
"I will send them to her and die";
And when the morning whitened
He left them where she went by.

She laid them upon her bosom,
Under a cloud of her hair,
And her red lips sang them a love-song,
Till stars grew out of the air.

She opened her door and her window,
And the heart and the soul came through,
To her right hand came the red one,
To her left hand came the blue.

They set up a noise like crickets,
A chattering wise and sweet,
And her hair was a folded flower
And the quiet of love in her feet.

W. B. YEATS

251 **A Slice of Wedding Cake**

Why have such scores of lovely, gifted girls
  Married impossible men?
Simple self-sacrifice may be ruled out,
  And missionary endeavour, nine times out of ten.

Repeat "impossible men": not merely rustic,
  Foul-tempered or depraved
(Dramatic foils chosen to show the world
  How well women behave, and always have behaved).

Impossible men: idle, illiterate,
  Self-pitying, dirty, sly,
For whose appearance even in City parks
  Excuses must be made to casual passers-by.

Has God's supply of tolerable husbands
  Fallen, in fact, so low?
Or do I always over-value woman
  At the expense of man?
                Do I?
                        It might be so.

ROBERT GRAVES

252 The Seeds of Love

I sowed the seeds of love
And I sowed them in the spring,
I gathered them up in the morning so soon
When the small birds sweetly sing.

My garden was planted well,
With flowers everywhere,
But I had not the liberty to choose for myself
The flower that I loved so dear.

The gardener standing by
I asked to choose for me –
He chose for me the violet, the lily and the pink,
But these I refused all three.

The violet I did not like
Because it fades so soon;
The lily and the pink I did overthink,
And vowed I would wait till June.

In June is the red, red rose,
And that is the flower for me:
I often times have plucked that red rose-bud
And gained the willow-tree.

The willow tree will twist,
And the willow tree will twine:
I wish I were in that young man's arms
That once had this heart of mine.

ANONYMOUS

253 The Parting

Since there's no help, come let us kiss and part –
Nay, I have done, you get no more of me;
And I am glad, yea, glad with all my heart,
That thus so cleanly I myself can free.
Shake hands for ever, cancel all our vows,
And when we meet at any time again,
Be it not seen in either of our brows
That we one jot of former love retain.
Now at the last gasp of Love's latest breath,
When, his pulse failing, Passion speechless lies,
When Faith is kneeling by his bed of death,
And Innocence is closing up his eyes,
– Now if thou wouldst, when all have given him over,
From death to life thou might'st him yet recover.

MICHAEL DRAYTON

254 When We Two Parted

When we two parted
In silence and tears,
Half broken-hearted
To sever for years,
Pale grew thy cheek and cold,
Colder thy kiss;
Truly that hour foretold
Sorrow to this.

The dew of the morning
   Sunk chill on my brow –
It felt like the warning
   Of what I feel now.
Thy vows are all broken,
   And light is thy fame:
I hear thy name spoken,
   And share in its shame.

They name thee before me,
   A knell to mine ear;
A shudder comes o'er me –
   Why wert thou so dear?
They know not I knew thee,
   Who knew thee too well:
Long, long shall I rue thee,
   Too deeply to tell.

In secret we met –
   In silence I grieve,
That thy heart could forget,
   Thy spirit deceive.
If I should meet thee
   After long years,
How could I greet thee?
   With silence and tears.

GEORGE GORDON BYRON

255 Song

The way of love was thus.
He was born one winter morn
With hands delicious,
And it was well with us.

Love came our quiet way,
Lit pride in us, and died in us,
All in a winter's day.
There is no more to say.

RUPERT BROOKE

256 Mariana

With blackest moss the flower-plots
  Were thickly crusted, one and all:
The rusted nails fell from the knots
  That held the pear to the gable-wall.
The broken sheds looked sad and strange:
  Unlifted was the clinking latch;
  Weeded and worn the ancient thatch
Upon the lonely moated grange.
    She only said, "My life is dreary,
      He cometh not," she said;
    She said, "I am aweary, aweary,
      I would that I were dead!"

Her tears fell with the dews at even;
  Her tears fell ere the dews were dried;
She could not look on the sweet heaven,
  Either at morn or eventide.
After the flitting of the bats,
  When thickest dark did trance the sky,
  She drew her casement-curtain by,
And glanced athwart the glooming flats.
    She only said, "The night is dreary,
      He cometh not," she said;
    She said, "I am aweary, aweary,
      I would that I were dead!"

Upon the middle of the night,
  Waking she heard the night-fowl crow:
The cock sung out an hour ere light:
  From the dark fen the oxen's low
Came to her: without hope of change,
  In sleep she seemed to walk forlorn,
  Till cold winds woke the gray-eyed morn
About the lonely moated grange.
    She only said, "The day is dreary,
      He cometh not," she said;
    She said, "I am aweary, aweary,
      I would that I were dead!"

About a stone-cast from the wall
  A sluice with blackened waters slept,
And o'er it many, round and small,
  The clustered marish-mosses crept.

Hard by a poplar shook alway,
  All silver-green with gnarlèd bark:
  For leagues no other tree did mark
The level waste, the rounding gray.
    She only said, "My life is dreary,
      He cometh not," she said;
    She said, "I am aweary, aweary,
      I would that I were dead!"

And ever when the moon was low,
  And the shrill winds were up and away,
In the white curtain, to and fro,
  She saw the gusty shadow sway.
But when the moon was very low,
  And wild winds bound within their cell,
  The shadow of the poplar fell
Upon her bed, across her brow.
    She only said, "The night is dreary,
      He cometh not," she said:
    She said, "I am aweary, aweary,
      I would that I were dead!"

All day within the dreamy house,
  The doors upon their hinges creaked;
The blue fly sung in the pane; the mouse
  Behind the mouldering wainscot shrieked,
Or from the crevice peered about.
  Old faces glimmered through the doors,
  Old footsteps trod the upper floors,
Old voices called her from without.

She only said, "My life is dreary,
He cometh not," she said;
She said, "I am aweary, aweary,
I would that I were dead!"

The sparrow's chirrup on the roof,
The slow clock ticking, and the sound
Which to the wooing wind aloof
The poplar made, did all confound
Her sense; but most she loathed the hour
When the thick-moted sunbeam lay
Athwart the chambers, and the day
Was sloping toward his western bower.
Then, said she, "I am very dreary,
He will not come," she said;
She wept, "I am aweary, aweary,
O God, that I were dead!"

ALFRED TENNYSON

257 To Marguerite

Yes! in the sea of life enisled,
With echoing straits between us thrown,
Dotting the shoreless watery wild,
We mortal millions live *alone*.
The islands feel the enclasping flow,
And then their endless bounds they know.

But when the moon their hollows lights,
And they are swept by balms of spring,
And in their glens, on starry nights,
The nightingales divinely sing;
And lovely notes, from shore to shore,
Across the sounds the channels pour;

O then a longing like despair
Is to their farthest caverns sent!
For surely once, they feel, we were
Parts of a single continent.
Now round us spreads the watery plain –
O might our marges meet again!

Who ordered that their longing's fire
Should be, as soon as kindled, cooled?
Who renders vain their deep desire? –
A God, a God their severance ruled!
And bade betwixt their shores to be
The unplumbed, salt, estranging sea.

MATTHEW ARNOLD

258 How Strangely This Sun

How strangely this sun reminds me of my love!
Of my walk alone at evening, when like the cottage
smoke
Hope vanished, written amongst red wastes of sky.
I remember my strained listening to his voice
My staring at his face and taking the photograph
With the river behind, and the woods touched by
Spring;
Till the identification of a morning –
Expansive sheets of blue rising from fields
Roaring movements of light observed under shadow –
With his figure leaning over a map, is now
complete.

What is left of that smoke which the wind blew
away?
I corrupted his confidence and his sunlike happiness
So that even now in his turning of bolts or driving a
machine
His hand will show error. That is for him.
For me this memory which now I behold,
When, from the pasturage, azure rounds me in rings
And the lark ascends, and his voice still rings, still
rings.

STEPHEN SPENDER

259 The End of a Leave

Out of the damp black light,
The noise of locomotives,
A thousand whispering,
Sharp-nailed, sinewed, slight,
I meet that alien thing
Your hand, with all its motives.

Far from the roof of night
And iron these encounter;
In the gigantic hall
As the severing light
Menaces, human, small,
These hands exchange their counters.

Suddenly our relation
Is terrifyingly simple
Against our wretched times,
Like a hand which mimes
Love in this anguished station
Against a whole world's pull.

ROY FULLER

260 **Absence**

Here, ever since you went abroad,
  If there be change, no change I see:
I only walk our wonted road,
  The road is only walked by me.

Yes; I forgot: a change there is –
  Was it of that you bade me tell?
I catch at times, at times I miss
  The sight, the tone, I know so well.

Only two months since you stood here?
  Two shortest months? Then tell me why
Voices are harsher than they were,
  And tears are longer ere they dry.

WALTER SAVAGE LANDOR

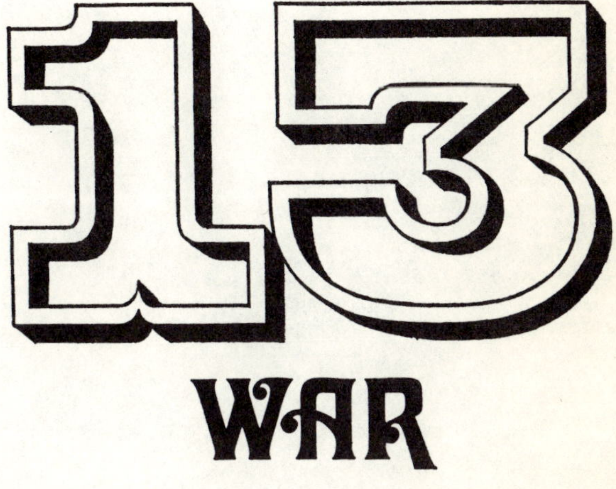

13 WAR

The struggle—which alone constitutes life for a poet—is to transmute his personal and private agonies into something rich and strange, something universal and impersonal.

T. S. Eliot

261 **Song**

Farewell, adieu, that court-like life!
  To war we 'tend to go:
It is good sport to see the strife
  Of soldiers on a row:
    How merrily they forward march
      Their enemies to slay!
    With hey trim and trixy too
      Their banners they display.

The drum and flute play lustily,
  The trumpet blows amain,
And vent'rous knights courageously
  Do march before their train,
    With spear in rest so lively dressed
      In armour bright and gay,
    With hey trim and trixy too
      Their banners they display.

JOHN PICKERING

262 The Destruction of Sennacherib

The Assyrian came down like the wolf on the fold,
And his cohorts were gleaming in purple and gold,
And the sheen of their spears was like stars on the sea,
When the blue wave rolls nightly on deep Galilee.

Like the leaves of the forest when summer is green,
That host, with their banners, at sunset were seen;
Like the leaves of the forest when autumn hath blown,
That host on the morrow lay withered and strown.

For the Angel of Death spread his wings on the blast,
And breathed in the face of the foe as he passed,
And the eyes of the sleepers waxed deadly and chill,
And their hearts but once heaved, and for ever grew
still.

And there lay the steed with his nostrils all wide,
But through them there rolled not the breath of his
pride,
And the foam of his gasping lay white on the turf
And cold as the spray of the rock-beating surf.

And there lay the rider distorted and pale,
With the dew on his brow, and the rust on his mail;
And the tents were all silent, the banners alone,
The lances uplifted, the trumpets unblown.

And the widows of Ashur are loud in their wail,
And the idols are broke in the temple of Baal;
And the might of the Gentile, unsmote by the sword,
Hath melted like snow in the glance of the Lord.

GEORGE GORDON BYRON

263 The War Song of Dinas Vawr

The mountain sheep are sweeter,
But the valley sheep are fatter;
We therefore deemed it meeter
To carry off the latter.
We made an expedition;
We met a host, and quelled it;
We forced a strong position,
And killed the men who held it.

On Dyfed's richest valley,
Where herds of kine were browsing,
We made a mighty sally,
To furnish our carousing.
Fierce warriors rushed to meet us;
We met them, and o'erthrew them:
They struggled hard to beat us;
But we conquered them, and slew them.

As we drove our prize at leisure,
The king marched forth to catch us:
His rage surpassed all measure,
But his people could not match us.
He fled to his hall-pillars;
And, ere our force we led off,
Some sacked his house and cellars,
While others cut his head off.

We there, in strife bewildering,
Spilt blood enough to swim in:
We orphaned many children,
And widowed many women.
The eagles and the ravens
We glutted with our foemen;
The heroes and the cravens,
The spearmen and the bowmen.

We brought away from battle,
And much their land bemoaned them,
Two thousand head of cattle,
And the head of him who owned them:
Ednyfed, King of Dyfed,
His head was borne before us;
His wine and beasts supplied our feasts,
And his overthrow, our chorus.

THOMAS LOVE PEACOCK

264 **Eager for Battle** (From *Henry IV Part I*)

Let them come.
They come like sacrifices in their trim,
And to the fire-eyed maid of smoky war,
All hot and bleeding, will we offer them.
The mailèd Mars shall on his altar sit
Up to the ears in blood. I am on fire
To hear this rich reprisal is so nigh,
And yet not ours. Come, let me taste my horse
Who is to bear me like a thunderbolt
Against the bosom of the Prince of Wales.

WILLIAM SHAKESPEARE

265 **Goliath**

Still as a mountain with dark pines and sun
He stood between the armies, and his shout
Rolled from the empyrean above the host:
"Bid any little flea ye have come forth,
And wince at death upon my finger-nail!"
He turned his large-boned face; and all his steel
Tossed into beams the lustre of the noon;
And all the shaggy horror of his locks
Rustled like locusts in a field of corn.
The meagre pupil of his shameless eye
Moved like a cormorant over a glassy sea.
He stretched his limbs, and laughed into the air,
To feel the growing sinews of his breast,
And the long gush of his swollen arteries pause:
And, nodding, wheeled, towering in all his height.
Then, like a wind that hushes, he gazed and saw
Down, down, far down upon the untroubled green
A shepherd-boy that swung a little sling.

Goliath shut his lids to drive that mote
Which vexed the eastern azure of his eye
Out of his vision; and stared down again.
Yet stood the youth there, ruddy in the flare
Of his vast shield, nor spake, nor quailed, gazed up,
As one might scan a mountain to be scaled.
Then, as it were, a voice unearthly still
Cried in the cavern of his bristling ear,
"His name is Death!" . . . And, like the flush
That dyes Sahara to its lifeless verge,
His brows' bright brass flamed into sudden crimson;

And his great spear leapt upward, lightning-like,
Shaking a dreadful thunder in the air;
Span betwixt earth and sky, bright as a berg
That hoards the sunlight in a myriad spires,
Crashed: and struck echo through an army's heart.

Then paused Goliath, and stared down again.
And fleet-foot Fear from rolling orbs perceived
Steadfast, unharmed, a stooping shepherd-boy
Frowning upon the target of his face.
And wrath tossed suddenly up once more his hand;
And a deep groan grieved all his strength in him.
He breathed; and, lost in dazzling darkness, prayed –
Besought his reins, his gloating gods, his youth:
And turned to smite what he no more could see.

Then sped the singing pebble-messenger,
The chosen of the Lord from Israel's brooks,
Fleet to its mark, and hollowed a light path
Down to the appalling Babel of his brain.
And like the smoke of dreaming Souffrière
Dust rose in cloud, spread wide, slow silted down
Softly all softly on his armour's blaze.

WALTER DE LA MARE

266 The Castle

All through that summer at ease we lay,
And daily from the turret wall
We watched the mowers in the hay
And the enemy half a mile away.
They seemed no threat to us at all.

For what, we thought, had we to fear
With our arms and provender, load on load,
Our towering battlements, tier on tier,
And friendly allies drawing near,
On every leafy summer road.

Our gates were strong, our walls were thick,
So smooth and high, no man could win
A foothold there, no clever trick
Could take us, have us dead or quick.
Only a bird could have got in.

What could they offer us for bait?
Our captain was brave and we were true . . .
There was a little private gate,
A little wicked wicket gate.
The wizened warder let them through.

O then our maze of tunnelled stone
Grew thin and treacherous as air.
The cause was lost without a groan,
The famous citadel overthrown,
And all its secret galleries bare.

How can this shameful tale be told?
I will maintain until my death
We could do nothing, being sold;
Our only enemy was gold,
And we had no arms to fight it with.

EDWIN MUIR

267 **In Prison**

Wearily, drearily,
Half the day long,
Flap the great banners
High over the stone;
Strangely and eerily
Sounds the wind's song,
Bending the banner-poles.

While, all alone,
Watching the loophole's spark,
Lie I, with life all dark,
Feet tethered, hands fettered
Fast to the stone,
The grim walls, square lettered
With prisoned men's groan.

Still strain the banner-poles
Through the wind's song,
Westward the banner rolls
Over my wrong.

WILLIAM MORRIS

268 On the Late Massacre in Piedmont

Avenge, O Lord, thy slaughtered saints, whose bones
  Lie scattered on the Alpine mountains cold;
  Even them who kept thy truth so pure of old,
  When all our fathers worshipped stocks and stones,
Forget not. In thy book record their groans
  Who were thy sheep, and in their ancient fold
  Slain by the bloody Piedmontese, that rolled
  Mother with infant down the rocks. Their moans
The vales redoubled to the hills, and they
  To heaven. Their martyred blood and ashes sow
  O'er all the Italian fields, where still doth sway
The triple tyrant; that from these may grow
  A hundredfold, who, having learnt thy way,
  Early may fly the Babylonian woe.

JOHN MILTON

269 **Ode**

How sleep the brave, who sink to rest
By all their country's wishes blest!
When Spring, with dewy fingers cold,
Returns to deck their hallowed mould,
She there shall dress a sweeter sod
Than Fancy's feet have ever trod.

By fairy hands their knell is rung;
By forms unseen their dirge is sung;
There Honour comes, a pilgrim gray,
To bless the turf that wraps their clay;
And Freedom shall awhile repair
To dwell, a weeping hermit, there!

WILLIAM COLLINS

270 **To Lucasta, Going to the War**

Tell me not, sweet, I am unkind,
  That from the nunnery
Of thy chaste breast and quiet mind
  To war and arms I fly.

True: a new Mistress now I chase,
  The first foe in the field;
And with a stronger faith embrace
  A sword, a horse, a shield.

Yet this inconstancy is such,
  As you too shall adore;
I could not love thee, dear, so much,
  Loved I not Honour more.

RICHARD LOVELACE

271 **The King Addresses His Army Before Battle** (From *Henry V*)

Once more unto the breach, dear friends, once more;
Or close the wall up with our English dead.
In peace there's nothing so becomes a man
As modest stillness and humility;
But when the blast of war blows in our ears,
Then imitate the action of the tiger;
Stiffen the sinews, summon up the blood,
Disguise fair nature with hard-favoured rage.

Then lend the eye a terrible aspect;
Let it pry through the portage of the head
Like the brass cannon; let the brow o'erwhelm it
As fearfully as does a gallèd rock
O'erhand and jutty his confounded base,
Swilled with the wild and wasteful ocean.
Now set the teeth, and stretch the nostril wide;
Hold hard the breath, and bend up every spirit
To his full height. On, on, you noble English,
Whose blood is fet from fathers of war-proof;
Fathers that, like so many Alexanders,
Have in these parts from morn till even fought,
And sheathed their swords for lack of argument.
Dishonour not your mothers; now attest
That those whom you called fathers did beget you.
Be copy now to men of grosser blood,
And teach them how to war. And you, good yeomen,
Whose limbs were made in England, show us here
The mettle of your pasture; let us swear
That you are worth your breeding, which I doubt not,
For there is none of you so mean and base,
That hath not noble lustre in your eyes.
I see you stand like greyhounds in the slips,
Straining upon the start. The game's afoot.
Follow your spirit, and upon this charge,
Cry "God for Harry, England and Saint George!"

WILLIAM SHAKESPEARE

272 An Irish Airman Foresees His Death

I know that I shall meet my fate
Somewhere among the clouds above;
Those that I fight I do not hate,
Those that I guard I do not love;
My country is Kiltartan Cross,
My countrymen Kiltartan's poor,
No likely end could bring them loss
Or leave them happier than before.
Nor law, nor duty bade me fight,
Nor public men, nor cheering crowds,
A lonely impulse of delight
Drove to this tumult in the clouds;
I balanced all, brought all to mind,
The years to come seemed waste of breath,
A waste of breath the years behind
In balance with this life, this death.

W. B. YEATS

273 When I Would Muse in Boyhood

When I would muse in boyhood
  The wild green woods among,
And nurse resolves and fancies
  Because the world was young,
It was not foes to conquer,
  Nor sweethearts to be kind,
But it was friends to die for
  That I would seek and find.

I sought them far and found them,
  The sure, the straight, the brave,
The hearts I lost my own to,
  The souls I could not save.
They braced their belts around them,
  They crossed in ships the sea,
They sought and found six feet of ground
  And there they died for me.

A. E. HOUSMAN

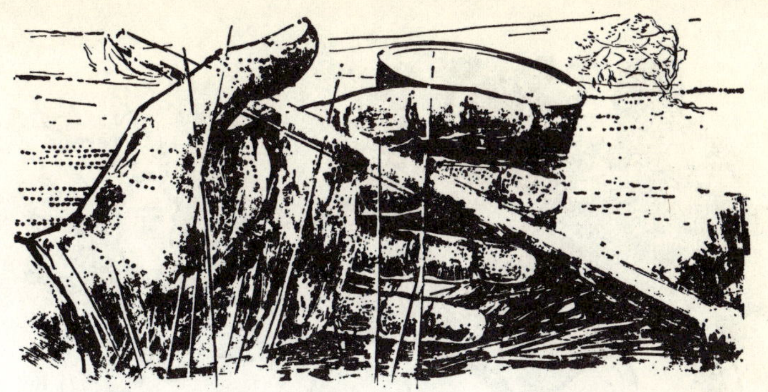

274 **Drummer Hodge**

They throw in Drummer Hodge, to rest
  Uncoffined – just as found:
His landmark is a kopje-crest
  That breaks the veldt around;
And foreign constellations west
  Each night above his mound.

Young Hodge the Drummer never knew –
  Fresh from his Wessex home –
The meaning of the broad Karoo,
  The bush, the dusty loam,
And why uprose to nightly view
  Strange stars amid the gloam.

Yet portion of that unknown plain
  Will Hodge for ever be;
His homely Northern breast and brain
  Grow to some Southern tree,
And strange-eyed constellations reign
  His stars eternally.

THOMAS HARDY

275 O What Is That Sound?

O what is that sound which so thrills the ear
  Down in the valley drumming, drumming?
Only the scarlet soldiers, dear,
    The soldiers coming.

O what is that light I see flashing so clear
  Over the distance brightly, brightly?
Only the sun on their weapons, dear,
    As they step lightly.

O what are they doing with all that gear;
  What are they doing this morning, this morning?
Only the usual manoeuvres, dear,
    Or perhaps a warning.

O why have they left the road down there;
  Why are they suddenly wheeling, wheeling?
Perhaps a change in the orders, dear;
    Why are you kneeling?

O haven't they stopped for the doctor's care;
  Haven't they reined their horses, their horses?
Why, they are none of them wounded, dear,
    None of these forces.

O is it the parson they want with white hair;
  Is it the parson, is it, is it?
No, they are passing his gateway, dear,
    Without a visit.

O it must be the farmer who lives so near;
  It must be the farmer so cunning, so cunning?
They have passed the farm already, dear,
    And now they are running.

O where are you going? stay with me here!
  Were the vows you swore me deceiving, deceiving?
No, I promised to love you, dear,
    But I must be leaving.

O it's broken the lock and splintered the door,
  O it's the gate where they're turning, turning;
Their feet are heavy on the floor
    And their eyes are burning.

W. H. AUDEN

276 War Poem

Don't stand at night by the gate, love,
He will not come again,
And there are eyes that laugh to see
The flowering of a pain.

Do not lay him a place, dear,
For you will eat alone;
Nor put you on that pretty dress,
The need for that is gone.

Just go into your room, lass,
And make yourself a prayer,
For that will be your strength now,
This many and many a year.

HENRY TREECE

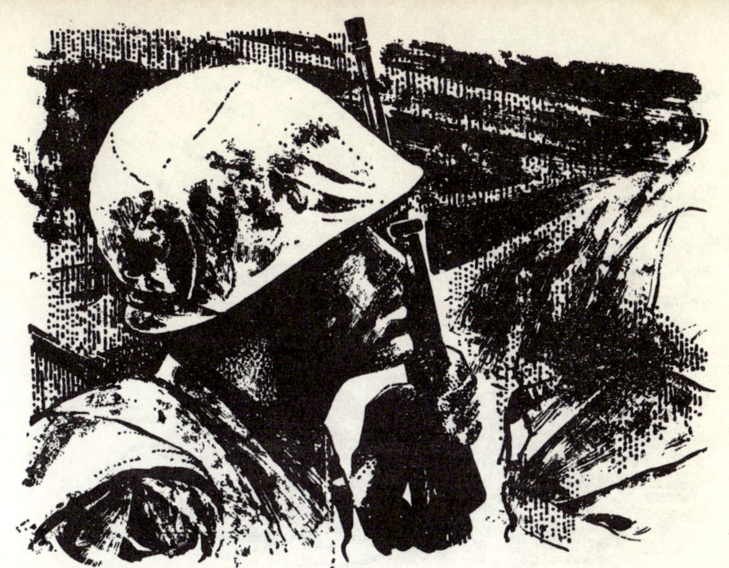

277 Anthem for Doomed Youth

What passing-bells for these who die as cattle?
Only the monstrous anger of the guns.
Only the stuttering rifles' rapid rattle
Can patter out their hasty orisons.
No mockeries for them from prayers or bells,
Nor any voice of mourning save the choirs, –
The shrill, demented choirs of wailing shells;
And bugles calling for them from sad shires.

What candles may be held to speed them all?
Not in the hands of boys, but in their eyes
Shall shine the holy glimmers of good-byes.
The pallor of girls' brows shall be their pall;
Their flowers the tenderness of silent minds,
And each slow dusk a drawing-down of blinds.

WILFRED OWEN

278 The Bay

The semi-circular and lunar bay
Where tumbling, grey stones meet untidily
The grey volcanic waves: no man, no tree,
Breaks the cold greenness of the bitten lea –
This scene the orator of memory
Already knew: forbore till now to say.

But on the hill the gun's black twig, the moan
Of the convoy home from seas instinct with steel,
The hidden spies, the bomber's slanting keel
As slowly it takes the wind – all these remain
Unwished, undreamed, unknown. They are the days,
The escaping seconds, terrible and real,
Through which I live; which memory will seal
To keep and smear for ever future bays.

ROY FULLER

279 Conquerors

By sundown we came to a hidden village
Where all the air was still
And no sound met our tired ears, save
For the sorry drip of rain from blackened trees
And the melancholy song of swinging gates.
Then through a broken pane some of us saw
A dead bird in a rusting cage, still
Pressing his thin tattered breast against the bars,
His beak wide open.   And
As we hurried through the weed-grown street,
A gaunt dog started up from some dark place
And shambled off on legs as thin as sticks
Into the wood, to die at least in peace.
No one had told us victory was like this;
Not one amongst us would have eaten bread
Before he'd filled the mouth of the grey child
That sprawled, stiff as a stone, before the shattered door.
There was not one who did not think of home.

HENRY TREECE

280 The Send-Off

Down the close, darkening lanes they sang their way
To the siding shed,
And lined the train with faces grimly gay.
Their breasts were stuck all white with wreath and spray
As men's are, dead.

Dull porters watched them, and a casual tramp
Stood staring hard,
Sorry to miss them from the upland camp.
Then, unmoved, signals nodded, and a lamp
Winked to the guard.

So secretly, like wrongs hushed-up, they went.
They were not ours:
We never heard to which front these were sent.
Nor there if they yet mock what women meant
Who gave them flowers.

Shall they return to beatings of great bells
In wild trainloads?
A few, a few, too few for drums and yells,
May creep back, silent, to still village wells
Up half-known roads.

WILFRED OWEN

281 **Naming of Parts**

To-day we have naming of parts. Yesterday,
We had daily cleaning. And to-morrow morning,
We shall have what to do after firing. But to-day,
To-day we have naming of parts. Japonica
Glistens like coral in all of the neighbouring gardens,
  And to-day we have naming of parts.

This is the lower sling swivel. And this
Is the upper sling swivel, whose use you will see,
When you are given your slings. And this is the
    piling swivel,
Which in your case you have not got. The branches
Hold in the gardens their silent, eloquent gestures,
  Which in our case we have not got.

This is the safety-catch, which is always released
With an easy flick of the thumb. And please do not let me
See anyone using his finger. You can do it quite easy
If you have any strength in your thumb. The blossoms
Are fragile and motionless, never letting anyone see
Any of them using their finger.

And this you can see is the bolt. The purpose of this
Is to open the breech, as you see. We can slide it
Rapidly backwards and forwards: we call this
Easing the spring. And rapidly backwards and forwards
The early bees are assaulting and fumbling the flowers:
They call it easing the Spring.

They call it easing the Spring: it is perfectly easy
If you have any strength in your thumb: like the bolt,
And the breech, and the cocking-piece, and the point of balance,
Which in our case we have not got; and the almond-blossom
Silent in all of the gardens and the bees going backwards and forwards,
For to-day we have naming of parts.

HENRY REED

282 All Day It Has Rained

All day it has rained, and we on the edge of the moors
Have sprawled in our bell-tents, moody and dull as
 boors,
Groundsheets and blankets spread on the muddy ground
And from the first grey wakening we have found
No refuge from the skirmishing fine rain
And the wind that made the canvas heave and flap
And the taut wet guy-ropes ravel out and snap.
All day the rain has glided, wave and mist and dream,
Drenching the gorse and heather, a gossamer stream
Too light to stir the acorns that suddenly
Snatched from their cups by the wild south-westerly
Pattered against the tent and our upturned dreaming
 faces.
And we stretched out, unbuttoning our braces,
Smoking a Woodbine, darning dirty socks,
Reading the Sunday papers – I saw a fox
And mentioned it in the note I scribbled home; –
And we talked of girls, and dropping bombs on Rome,
And thought of the quiet dead and the loud celebrities
Exhorting us to slaughter, and the herded refugees;
– Yet thought softly, morosely of them, and as
 indifferently
As of ourselves or those whom we
For years have loved, and will again
Tomorrow maybe love; but now it is the rain
Possesses us entirely, the twilight and the rain.

And I can remember nothing dearer or more to my
 heart
Than the children I watched in the woods on Saturday

Shaking down burning chestnuts for the schoolyard's
  merry play,
Or the shaggy patient dog who followed me
By Sheet and Steep and up the wooded scree
To the Shoulder o' Mutton where Edward Thomas
  brooded long
On death and beauty – till a bullet stopped his song.

ALUN LEWIS

283 **Will It Be So Again?**

Will it be so again
That the brave, the gifted are lost from view,
And the empty, scheming men
Are left in peace their lunatic age to renew?
Will it be so again?

Must it be always so
That the best are chosen to fall and sleep
Like seeds, and we too slow
In claiming the earth they quicken, and the old
  usurpers reap
What they could not sow?

Will it be so again –
The jungle code and the hypocrite gesture?
A poppy wreath for the slain
And a cut-throat world for the living? that stale imposture
Played on us once again?

Will it be as before –
Peace, with no heart or mind to ensure it,
Guttering down to war
Like a libertine to his grave? We should not be surprised: we knew it
Happen before.

Shall it be so again?
Call not upon the glorious dead
To be your witnesses then.
The living alone can nail to their promise the ones who said
It shall not be so again.

C. DAY LEWIS

284 **In the Pink**

So Davies wrote: "This leaves me in the pink".
Then scrawled his name: "Your loving sweetheart,
 Willie".
With crosses for a hug. He'd had a drink
Of rum and tea; and, though the barn was chilly,
For once his blood ran warm; he had pay to spend.
Winter was passing; soon the year would mend.

But he couldn't sleep that night; stiff in the dark
He groaned and thought of Sundays at the farm,
And how he'd go as cheerful as a lark
In his best suit, to wander arm in arm
With brown-eyed Gwen, and whisper in her ear
The simple, silly things she liked to hear.

And then he thought; to-morrow night we trudge
Up to the trenches, and my boots are rotten.
Five miles of stodgy clay and freezing sludge,
And everything but wretchedness forgotten.
To-night he's in the pink; but soon he'll die.
And still the war goes on – *he* don't know why.

SIEGFRIED SASSOON

285 **Strange Meeting**

It seemed that out of battle I escaped
Down some profound dull tunnel, long since scooped
Through granites which titanic wars had groined.
Yet also there encumbered sleepers groaned,
Too fast in thought or death to be bestirred.
Then, as I probed them, one sprang up, and stared
With piteous recognition in fixed eyes,
Lifting distressful hands as if to bless.
And by his smile, I knew that sullen hall,
By his dead smile I knew we stood in Hell.
With a thousand pains that vision's face was grained;
Yet no blood reached there from the upper ground,
And no guns thumped, or down the flues made moan.
"Strange friend," I said, "here is no cause to mourn."
"None," said the other, "save the undone years,
The hopelessness. Whatever hope is yours,

Was my life also; I went hunting wild
After the wildest beauty in the world,
Which lies not calm in eyes, or braided hair,
But mocks the steady running of the hour,
And if it grieves, grieves richlier than here.
For by my glee might many men have laughed,
And of my weeping something had been left,
Which must die now. I mean the truth untold,
The pity of war, the pity war distilled.
Now men will go content with what we spoiled.
Or, discontent, boil bloody, and be spilled.
They will be swift with swiftness of the tigress,
None will break ranks, though nations trek from
progress.
Courage was mine, and I had mystery,
Wisdom was mine, and I had mastery;
To miss the march of this retreating world
Into vain citadels that are not walled.
Then, when much blood had clogged their
chariot-wheels
I would go up and wash them from sweet wells,
Even with truths that lie too deep for taint.
I would have poured my spirit without stint
But not through wounds; not on the cess of war.
Foreheads of men have bled where no wounds were.
I am the enemy you killed, my friend.
I knew you in this dark; for so you frowned
Yesterday through me as you jabbed and killed.
I parried; but my hands were loath and cold.
Let us sleep now. . . ."

WILFRED OWEN

286 **Futility**

Move him into the sun –
Gently its touch awoke him once,
At home, whispering of fields unsown.
Always it woke him, even in France,
Until this morning and this snow.
If anything might rouse him now
The kind old sun will know.

Think how it wakes the seeds, –
Woke, once, the clays of a cold star.
Are limbs, so dear achieved, are sides,
Full-nerved – still warm – too hard to stir?
Was it for this the clay grew tall?
– O what made fatuous sunbeams toil
To break earth's sleep at all?

WILFRED OWEN

Poetry is not concerned with telling people what to do, but with extending our knowledge of good and evil, perhaps making the necessity for action more urgent and its nature more clear, but only leading us to the point where it is possible to make a rational and moral choice.

W. H. Auden

287 **Virtue**

Sweet day, so cool, so calm, so bright,
The bridal of the earth and sky,
The dew shall weep thy fall to-night;
For thou must die.

Sweet rose, whose hue angry and brave
Bids the rash gazer wipe his eye,
Thy root is ever in its grave,
And thou must die.

Sweet spring, full of sweet days and roses,
A box where sweets compacted lie,
My music shows ye have your closes,
And all must die.

Only a sweet and virtuous soul,
Like seasoned timber, never gives;
But though the whole world turn to coal,
Then chiefly lives.

GEORGE HERBERT

288 The Man of Life Upright

The man of life upright,
  Whose guiltless heart is free
From all dishonest deeds,
  Or thought of vanity;

The man whose silent days
  In harmless joys are spent,
Whom hopes cannot delude,
  Nor sorrow discontent;

That man needs neither towers
  Nor armour for defence,
Nor secret vaults to fly
  From thunder's violence.

He only can behold
  With unaffrighted eyes
The horrors of the deep
  And terrors of the skies.

Thus, scorning all the cares
  That fate or fortune brings,
He makes the heaven his book,
  His wisdom heavenly things;

Good thoughts his only friends,
  His wealth a well-spent age,
The earth his sober inn
  And quiet pilgrimage.

THOMAS CAMPION

289 The Quiet Mind

Sweet are the thoughts that savour of content,
The quiet mind is richer than a crown;
Sweet are the nights in careless slumber spent,
The poor estate scorns fortune's angry frown:
Such sweet content, such minds, such sleep, such bliss,
Beggars enjoy, when princes oft do miss.

The homely house that harbours quiet rest,
The cottage that affords no pride nor care,
The mean that agrees with country music best,
The sweet consort of mirth and music's fare,
Obscurèd life sets down a type of bliss;
A mind content both crown and kingdom is.

ROBERT GREENE

290 Mercy (From *The Merchant of Venice*)

The quality of mercy is not strained,
It droppeth as the gentle rain from heaven
Upon the place beneath. It is twice blest;
It blesseth him that gives, and him that takes.
'Tis mightiest in the mightiest. It becomes
The thronèd monarch better than his crown;
His sceptre shows the force of temporal power,
The attribute to awe and majesty,
Wherein doth sit the dread and fear of kings;
But mercy is above this sceptred sway,
It is enthronèd in the hearts of kings,
It is an attribute to God himself . . .

WILLIAM SHAKESPEARE

291 The Little Black Boy

My mother bore me in the southern wild,
  And I am black, but O, my soul is white!
White as an angel is the English child,
  But I am black, as if bereaved of light.

My mother taught me underneath a tree,
  And, sitting down before the heat of day,
She took me on her lap and kissèd me,
  And, pointing to the east, began to say:

"Look at the rising sun: there God does live,
  And gives His light, and gives His heat away;
And flowers and trees and beasts and men receive
  Comfort in morning, joy in the noonday.

"And we are put on earth a little space,
  That we may learn to bear the beams of love;
And these black bodies and this sunburnt face
  Are but a cloud, and like a shady grove.

"For when our souls have learned the heat to bear,
  The cloud will vanish, we shall hear His voice,
Saying, 'Come out from the grove, my love and care,
  And round my golden tent like lambs rejoice.' "

Thus did my mother say, and kissèd me;
  And thus I say to little English boy.
When I from black and he from white cloud free,
  And round the tent of God like lambs we joy,

I'll shade him from the heat. till he can bear
   To lean in joy upon our Father's knee:
And then I'll stand and stroke his silver hair,
   And be like him, and he will then love me.

WILLIAM BLAKE

292 **And Did Those Feet in Ancient Time**

And did those feet in ancient time
  Walk upon England's mountains green?
And was the holy Lamb of God
  On England's pleasant pastures seen?

And did the countenance divine
  Shine forth upon our clouded hills?
And was Jerusalem builded here
  Among these dark Satanic mills?

Bring me my bow of burning gold!
  Bring me my arrows of desire!
Bring me my spear! O clouds, unfold!
  Bring me my chariot of fire!

I will not cease from mental fight,
  Nor shall my sword sleep in my hand,
Till we have built Jerusalem
  In England's green and pleasant land.

WILLIAM BLAKE

293 **East London**

'Twas August, and the fierce sun overhead
Smote on the squalid streets of Bethnal Green,
And the pale weaver, through his windows seen
In Spitalfields, looked thrice dispirited.
I met a preacher there I knew, and said:
"Ill and o'erworked, how fare you in this scene?" –
"Bravely!" said he; "for I of late have been
Much cheered with thoughts of Christ, *the living bread.*"

O human soul! as long as thou canst so
Set up a mark of everlasting light,
Above the howling senses' ebb and flow,
To cheer thee, and to right thee if thou roam –
Not with lost toil thou labourest through the night!
Thou mak'st the heaven thou hop'st indeed thy home.

MATTHEW ARNOLD

294 As I Came Home from Labour

As I came home from labour,
So stiff with sweat and pain,
I heard two starlings singing
Above the long pit-lane.

Their songs were all of summer,
And hope and love lives yet;
But I was sick and weary
And stiff with pain and sweat.

They sing, thought I, of pleasure,
And pain is never done;
They sing of ease and comfort,
And comfort I have none.

There's naught for folk who labour
But misery and rue;
No ease is theirs, no solace,
No hope the whole world through.

And there I lingered grieving,
And heard those happy songs,
And thought of all who labour
And bear their bitter wrongs.

F. C. BODEN

295 Art Thou Poor?

Art thou poor, yet has thou golden slumbers?
    O sweet content!
Art thou rich, yet is thy mind perplexèd?
    O punishment!
Dost thou laugh to see how fools are vexèd
To add to golden numbers, golden numbers?
O sweet content! O sweet, O sweet content!
  Work apace, apace, apace, apace;
  Honest labour bears a lovely face;
Then hey nonny nonny, hey nonny nonny!

Canst drink the waters of the crispèd spring?
    O sweet content!
Swimm'st thou in wealth, yet sink'st in thine own
  tears?
    O punishment!
Then he that patiently want's burden bears,
No burden bears, but is a king, a king!
O sweet content! O sweet, O sweet content!
  Work apace, apace, apace, apace;
  Honest labour bears a lovely face;
Then hey nonny nonny, hey nonny nonny!

THOMAS DEKKER

296 A Father's Advice to His Son

(From *Hamlet*)

Give thy thought no tongue,
Nor any unproportioned thought his act.
Be thou familiar, but by no means vulgar.
The friends thou hast, and their adoption tried,
Grapple them to thy soul with hoops of steel;
But do not dull thy palm with entertainment
Of each new-hatched, unfledged comrade. Beware
Of entrance to a quarrel; but being in,
Bear't, that th'opposed may beware of thee.
Give every man thine ear, but few thy voice;
Take each man's censure, but reserve thy judgement.
Costly thy habit as thy purse can buy,
But not expressed in fancy; rich, not gaudy;
For the apparel oft proclaims the man. . . .
Neither a borrower, nor a lender be,
For loan oft loses both itself and friend,
And borrowing dulls the edge of husbandry.
This above all: to thine own self be true,
And it must follow, as the night the day,
Thou canst not then be false to any man.

WILLIAM SHAKESPEARE

297 If –

If you can keep your head when all about you
  Are losing theirs and blaming it on you;
If you can trust yourself when all men doubt you,
  But make allowance for their doubting too;
If you can wait and not be tired by waiting,
  Or being lied about, don't deal in lies,
Or being hated, don't give way to hating,
  And yet don't look too good, nor talk too wise;

If you can dream – and not make dreams your master;
  If you can think – and not make thoughts your aim;
If you can meet with Triumph and Disaster
  And treat those two impostors just the same;
If you can bear to hear the truth you've spoken
  Twisted by knaves to make a trap for fools,
Or watch the things you gave your life to, broken,
  And stoop and build 'em up with worn-out tools;

If you can make one heap of all your winnings
  And risk it on one turn of pitch-and-toss,
And lose, and start again at your beginnings,
  And never breathe a word about your loss;
If you can force your heart and nerve and sinew
  To serve your turn long after they are gone,
And so hold on when there is nothing in you
  Except the Will which says to them: "Hold on!"

If you can talk with crowds and keep your virtue,
  Or walk with Kings – nor lose the common touch;
If neither foes nor loving friends can hurt you;
  If all men count with you, but none too much;
If you can fill the unforgiving minute
  With sixty seconds' worth of distance run,
Yours is the Earth and everything that's in it,
  And – which is more – you'll be a Man, my son!

RUDYARD KIPLING

298 Abou Ben Adhem

Abou Ben Adhem (may his tribe increase!)
Awoke one night from a deep dream of peace,
And saw, within the moonlight in his room,
Making it rich, and like a lily in bloom,
An angel writing in a book of gold: –
Exceeding peace had made Ben Adhem bold,
And to the presence in the room he said,
"What writest thou?" – The vision raised its head,
And with a look made of all sweet accord,
Answered, "The names of those who love the Lord."

"And is mine one?" said Abou. "Nay, not so,"
Replied the angel. Abou spoke more low,
But cheerly still; and said, "I pray thee, then,
Write me as one that loves his fellow-men."
The angel wrote, and vanished. The next night
It came again with a great wakening light,
And showed the names whom love of God had blessed,
And lo! Ben Adhem's name led all the rest.

LEIGH HUNT

299 The Road Not Taken

Two roads diverged in a yellow wood,
And sorry I could not travel both
And be one traveller, long I stood
And looked down one as far as I could
To where it bent in the undergrowth;

Then took the other, as just as fair,
And having perhaps the better claim,
Because it was grassy and wanted wear;
Though as for that the passing there
Had worn them really about the same,

And both that morning equally lay
In leaves no step had trodden black.
Oh, I kept the first for another day!
Yet knowing how way leads on to way,
I doubted if I should ever come back.

I shall be telling this with a sigh
Somewhere ages and ages hence:
Two roads diverged in a wood, and I –
I took the one less travelled by,
And that has made all the difference.

ROBERT FROST

300 **Ozymandias**

I met a traveller from an antique land
Who said: Two vast and trunkless legs of stone
Stand in the desert . . . Near them, on the sand,
Half sunk, a shattered visage lies, whose frown
And wrinkled lip, and sneer of cold command,
Tell that its sculptor well those passions read
Which yet survive, stamped on these lifeless things,
The hand that mocked them, and the heart that fed:
And on the pedestal these words appear:
"My name is Ozymandias, king of kings:
Look on my works, ye Mighty, and despair!"
Nothing beside remains. Round the decay
Of that colossal wreck, boundless and bare
The lone and level sands stretch far away.

PERCY BYSSHE SHELLEY

301 **I Think Continually . . .**

I think continually of those who were truly great.
Who, from the womb, remembered the soul's history
Through corridors of light where the hours are suns,
Endless and singing. Whose lovely ambition
Was that their lips, still touched with fire,
Should tell of the Spirit, clothed from head to foot in
song.
And who hoarded from the Spring branches
The desires falling across their bodies like blossoms.

What is precious is never to forget
The essential delight of the blood drawn from ageless
springs
Breaking through rocks in worlds before our earth.
Never to deny its pleasure in the morning simple light
Nor its grave evening demand for love.
Never to allow gradually the traffic to smother
With noise and fog, the flowering of the Spirit.

Near the snow, near the sun, in the highest fields
See how these names are fêted by the waving grass
And by the streamers of white cloud
And whispers of wind in the listening sky.
The names of those who in their lives fought for life,
Who wore at their hearts the fire's centre.
Born of the sun, they travelled a short while toward the
sun,
And left the vivid air signed with their honour.

STEPHEN SPENDER

302 To a Friend Whose Work Has Come to Nothing

Now all the truth is out,
Be secret and take defeat
From any brazen throat,
For how can you compete,
Being honour bred, with one
Who, were it proved he lies,
Were neither shamed in his own
Nor in his neighbour's eyes?
Bred to a harder thing
Than Triumph, turn away
And like a laughing string
Whereon mad fingers play
Amid a place of stone,
Be secret and exult,
Because of all things known
That is most difficult.

W. B. YEATS

303 **All the Facts**

A shilling life will give you all the facts:
How Father beat him, how he ran away,
What were the struggles of his youth, what acts
Made him the greatest figure of his day:
Of how he fought, fished, hunted, worked all night,
Though giddy, climbed new mountains; named a sea:
Some of the last researchers even write
Love made him weep his pints like you and me.

With all his honours on, he sighed for one
Who, say astonished critics, lived at home;
Did little jobs about the house with skill
And nothing else; could whistle; would sit still
Or potter round the garden; answered some
Of his long marvellous letters but kept none.

W. H. AUDEN

304 The World

The world is too much with us; late and soon,
   Getting and spending, we lay waste our powers:
   Little we see in Nature that is ours;
We have given our hearts away, a sordid boon!
This sea that bares her bosom to the moon;
   The winds that will be howling at all hours,
   And are up-gathered now like sleeping flowers;
For this, for everything, we are out of tune;
It moves us not. – Great God! I'd rather be
   A Pagan suckled in a creed outworn;
So might I, standing on this pleasant lea,
   Have glimpses that would make me less forlorn;
Have sight of Proteus rising from the sea;
   Or hear old Triton blow his wreathèd horn.

WILLIAM WORDSWORTH

305 Waiting Both

A star looks down at me,
And says: "Here I and you
Stand, each in our degree:
What do you mean to do, –
   Mean to do?"

I say: "For all I know,
Wait, and let Time go by,
Till my change come." – "Just so,"
The star says: "So mean I: –
   So mean I."

THOMAS HARDY

306 **Acquainted with the Night**

I have been one acquainted with the night.
I have walked out in rain – and back in rain.
I have outwalked the furthest city light.

I have looked down the saddest city lane.
I have passed by the watchman on his beat
And dropped my eyes, unwilling to explain.

I have stood still and stopped the sound of feet
When far away an interrupted cry
Came over houses from another street,

But not to call me back or say good-bye;
And further still at an unearthly height,
One luminary clock against the sky

Proclaimed the time was neither wrong nor right.
I have been one acquainted with the night.

ROBERT FROST

307 **Peace**

My soul, there is a country
  Far beyond the stars,
Where stands a wingèd sentry
  All skilful in the wars:

There, above noise and danger,
  Sweet Peace sits crowned with smiles,
And One born in a manger
  Commands the beauteous files.

He is thy gracious Friend,
  And – O my soul, awake! –
Did in pure love descend,
  To die here for thy sake.

If thou canst get but thither,
  There grows the flower of Peace,
The Rose that cannot wither,
  Thy fortress, and thy ease.

Leave then thy foolish ranges,
  For none can thee secure
But One who never changes,
  Thy God, thy life, thy cure.

HENRY VAUGHAN

308 **On His Blindness**

When I consider how my light is spent,
Ere half my days, in this dark world and wide,
And that one Talent which is death to hide,
Lodged with me useless, though my Soul more bent
To serve therewith my Maker, and present
My true account, lest he returning chide;
Doth God exact day-labour, light denied,
I fondly ask; But patience, to prevent
That murmur, soon replies, God doth not need
Either man's work or his own gifts; who best
Bear his mild yoke, they serve him best, his State
Is Kingly. Thousands at his bidding speed
And post o'er Land and Ocean without rest:
They also serve who only stand and wait.

JOHN MILTON

309 Out of the Night That Covers Me

Out of the night that covers me,
  Black as the pit from pole to pole,
I thank whatever gods may be
  For my unconquerable soul.

In the fell clutch of circumstance
  I have not winced nor cried aloud.
Under the bludgeonings of chance
  My head is bloody, but unbowed.

Beyond this place of wrath and tears
  Looms but the Horror of the shade,
And yet the menace of the years
  Finds, and shall find me, unafraid.

It matters not how strait the gate,
  How charged with punishments the scroll,
I am the master of my fate;
  I am the captain of my soul.

W. E. HENLEY

310 **The World**

I saw Eternity the other night
Like a great *Ring* of pure and endless light,
  All calm, as it was bright;
And round beneath it, Time in hours, days, years,
    Driven by the spheres
Like a vast shadow moved; in which the world
    And all her train were hurled.
The doting lover in his quaintest strain
    Did there complain;
Near him, his lute, his fancy and his flights,
    Wit's sour delights:
With gloves and knots, the silly snares of pleasure,
    Yet his dear treasure
All scattered lay, while he his eyes did pour
    Upon a flower.

The darksome statesman, hung with weights and woe,
Like a thick midnight fog, moved there so slow,
  He did not stay, nor go;
Condemning thoughts – like sad eclipses – scowl
    Upon his soul,
And clouds of crying witnesses without
    Pursued him with one shout.
Yet digged the mole, and lest his ways be found,
    Worked under ground,
Where he did clutch his prey; but one did see
    That policy:
Churches and altars fed him; perjuries
    Were gnats and flies;
It rained about him blood and tears, but he
    Drank them as free.

The fearful miser on a heap of rust
Sat pining all his life there, did scarce trust
 His own hands with the dust,
Yet would not place one piece above, but lives
  In fear of thieves.
Thousands there were as frantic as himself,
  And hugged each one his pelf;
And downright epicure placed heaven in sense,
  And scorned pretence;
While others, slipped into a wide excess,
  Said little less;
The weaker sort slight, trivial wares enslave,
  Who think them brave;
And poor, despisèd Truth sat counting by
  Their victory.

Yet some, who all this while did weep and sing,
And sing and weep, soared up into the Ring;
 But most would use no wing.
O fools – said I – thus to prefer dark night
  Before true light!
To live in grots and caves, and hate the day
  Because it shows the way;
The way, which from this dead and dark abode
  Leads up to God;
A way where you might tread the sun, and be
  More bright than he!
But as I did their madness so discuss,
  One whispered thus,
This Ring the Bridegroom did for none provide,
  But for his bride.

HENRY VAUGHAN

311 At a Lunar Eclipse

Thy shadow, Earth, from Pole to Central Sea,
Now steals along upon the Moon's meek shine
In even monochrome and curving line
Of imperturbable serenity.

How shall I link such sun-cast symmetry
With the torn troubled form I know as thine,
That profile, placid as a brow divine,
With continents of moil and misery?

And can immense Mortality but throw
So small a shade, and Heaven's high human scheme
Be hemmed within the coasts yon arc implies?

Is such the stellar gauge of earthly show,
Nation at war with nation, brains that teem,
Heroes, and women fairer than the skies?

THOMAS HARDY

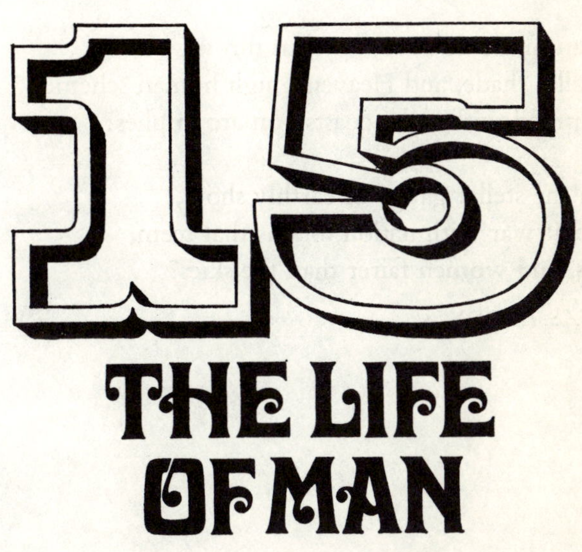

The poet, described in ideal perfection, brings the whole soul of man into activity.

Samuel Taylor Coleridge

312 **The Ages of Man** (From *As You Like It*)

All the world's a stage,
And all the men and women merely players:
They have their exits and their entrances;
And one man in his time plays many parts,
His acts being seven ages. At first the infant
Mewling and puking in the nurse's arms.
And then the whining schoolboy, with his satchel
And shining morning face, creeping like snail
Unwillingly to school. And then the lover,
Sighing like a furnace, with a woeful ballad
Made to his mistress' eyebrow. Then a soldier
Full of strange oaths, and bearded like the pard,
Jealous in honour, sudden and quick in quarrel,
Seeking the bubble reputation
Even in the cannon's mouth. And then the justice,
In fair round belly with good capon lined,
With eyes severe, and beard of formal cut,
Full of wise saws and modern instances;
And so he plays his part. The sixth age shifts
Into the lean and slippered pantaloon,
With spectacles on nose and pouch on side;
His youthful hose well saved a world too wide
For his shrunk shank; and his big manly voice,
Turning again towards childish treble, pipes
And whistles in his sound. Last scene of all,
That ends this strange eventful history,
In second childishness, and mere oblivion,
Sans teeth, sans eyes, sans taste, sans everything.

WILLIAM SHAKESPEARE

313 Prayer before Birth

I am not yet born; O hear me.
Let not the bloodsucking bat or the rat or the stoat or
the club-footed ghoul come near me.

I am not yet born; console me.
I fear that the human race may with tall walls wall me,
with strong drugs dope me, with wise lies lure me,
on black racks rack me, in blood-baths roll me.

I am not yet born; provide me
With water to dandle me, grass to grow for me, tree to talk
to me, sky to sing to me, birds and a white light
in the back of my mind to guide me.

I am not yet born; forgive me
For the sins that in me the world shall commit, my words
when they speak me, my thought when they think me,
my treason engendered by traitors beyond me,
my life when they murder by means of my
hands, my death when they live me.

I am not yet born; rehearse me
In the parts I must play and the cues I must take when
old men lecture me, bureaucrats hector me,
mountains frown on me, lovers laugh at me, the
white waves call me to folly and the desert calls
me to doom and the beggar refuses
my gift and my children curse me.

I am not yet born; O hear me,
Let not the man who is beast or who thinks he is God
come near me.

I am not yet born; O fill me
With strength against those who would freeze my
humanity, would dragoon me into a lethal automaton,
would make me a cog in a machine, a thing with
one face, a thing, and against all those
who would dissipate my entirety, would
blow me like thistledown hither and
thither or hither and thither
like water held in the
hands would spill me.
Let them not make a stone and let them not spill me.
Otherwise kill me.

LOUIS MACNEICE

314 A Carol

O hush thee, my baby,
Thy cradle's in pawn:
No blankets to cover thee
Cold and forlorn.
The stars in the bright sky
Look down and are dumb
At the heir of the ages
Asleep in a slum.

The hooters are blowing,
No heed let him take;
When baby is hungry
'Tis best not to wake.
Thy mother is crying,
Thy dad's on the dole:
Two shillings a week is
The price of a soul.

C. DAY LEWIS

315 The Piper's Song

Piping down the valleys wild,
  Piping songs of pleasant glee,
On a cloud I saw a child,
  And he laughing said to me:

"Pipe a song about a lamb!"
  So I piped with merry cheer.
"Piper, pipe that song again!"
  So I piped; he wept to hear.

"Drop thy pipe, thy happy pipe;
  Sing thy songs of happy cheer!"
So I sang the same again,
  While he wept with joy to hear.

"Piper, sit thee down and write
  In a book that all may read!"
So he vanished from my sight;
  And I plucked a hollow reed,

And I made a rural pen,
  And I stained the water clear,
And I wrote my happy songs
  Every child may joy to hear.

WILLIAM BLAKE

316 **Baby Running Barefoot**

When the white feet of the baby beat across the grass
The little white feet nod like white flowers in a wind,
They poise and run like puffs of wind that pass
Over water where the weeds are thinned,

And the sight of their white playing in the grass
Is winsome as a robin's song, so fluttering;
Or like two butterflies that settle on a glass
Cup for a moment, soft little wing-beats uttering.

And I wish that the baby would tack across here to me
Like a wind-shadow running on a pond, so she could
  stand
With two little bare white feet upon my knee
And I could feel her feet in either hand

Cool as syringa buds in morning hours,
Or firm and silken as young peony flowers.

D. H. LAWRENCE

317 **Children Who Were Rough**

My parents kept me from children who were rough
And who threw words like stones and who wore torn
clothes.
Their thighs showed through rags. They ran in the
street
And climbed cliffs and stripped by the country streams.

I feared more than tigers their muscles like iron
Their jerking hands and their knees tight on my arms.
I feared the salt coarse pointing of those boys
Who copied my lisp behind me on the road.

They were lithe, they sprang out behind hedges
Like dogs to bark at our world. They threw mud
And I looked another way, pretending to smile.
I longed to forgive them, yet they never smiled.

STEPHEN SPENDER

318 **The Belfry**

Dark is the stair, and humid the old walls
Wherein it winds, on worn stones, up the tower.
Only by loophole chinks at intervals
Pierces the late glow of this August hour.

Two truant children climb the stairway dark,
With joined hands, half in glee and half in fear;
The boy mounts brisk, the girl hangs back to hark
If the gruff sexton their light footsteps hear.

Dazzled at last they gain the belfry-room.
Barred rays through shutters hover across the floor,
Dancing in dust; so fresh they come from gloom
That breathless they pause wondering at the door.

How hushed it is! What smell of timbers old
From cobwebbed beams! The warm light here and
  there
Edging a darkness, sleeps in pools of gold,
Or weaves fantastic shadows through the air.

How motionless the huge bell! Straight and stiff,
Ropes through the floor rise to the rafters dim.
The shadowy round of metal hangs, as if
No force could ever lift its gleamy rim.

A child's awe, a child's wonder – who shall trace
What dumb thoughts on its waxen softness write
In such a spell-brimmed, time-forgotten place,
Bright in that strangeness of approaching night?

As these two gaze, their fingers tighter press;
For suddenly the low bell upward heaves
Its vast mouth, the cords quiver at the stress,
And ere the heart prepare, the ear receives

Full on its delicate sense the plangent stroke
Of violent, iron, reverberating sound.
As if the tower in all its stones awoke,
Deep echoes tremble, again in clangour drowned,

That starts without a whir of frightened wings
And holds the young hearts shaken, hushed and
   thrilled,
Like frail reeds in a rushing stream, like strings
Of music, or like trees with tempest filled,

And rolls in wide waves out o'er the lone land,
Tone following tone toward the far-setting sun,
Till where in fields long-shadowed reapers stand,
Bowed heads look up, and lo, the day is done.

LAURENCE BINYON

319 **By St Thomas Water**

By St Thomas Water
Where the river is thin
We looked for a jam-jar
To catch the quick fish in.
Through St Thomas Church-yard
Jessie and I ran
The day we took the jam-pot
Off the dead man.

On the scuffed tombstone
The grey flowers fell,
Cracked was the water,
Silent the shell.
The snake was an emblem
Swirled on the slab,
Across the beach of sky the sun
Crawled like a crab.

"If we walk," said Jessie,
"Seven times round,
We shall hear a dead man
Speaking underground."
Round the stone we danced, we sang,
Watched the sun drop,
Laid our heads and listened
At the tomb-top.

Soft as the thunder
At the storm's start
I heard a voice as clear as blood,
Strong as the heart.
But what words were spoken
I can never say,
I shut my fingers round my head,
Drove them away.

"Jessie, what are those letters
Cut so sharp and trim
All round this holy stone
With earth up to the brim?"
Jessie traced the letters
Black as coffin-lead.
"*He is not dead but sleeping,*"
Slowly she said.

I looked at Jessie,
Jessie looked at me,
And our eyes in wonder
Grew wide as the sea.

Past the green and bending stones
We fled hand in hand,
Silent through the tongues of grass
To the river strand.

By the creaking cypress
We moved as soft as smoke
For fear all the people
Underneath awoke.
Over all the sleepers
We darted light as snow
In case they opened up their eyes,
Called us from below.

Many a day has faltered
Into many a year
Since the dead awoke and spoke
And we would not hear.
Waiting in the cold grass
Under a crinkled bough,
Quiet stone, cautious stone,
What do you tell me now?

CHARLES CAUSLEY

320 **Mermaid, Dragon, Fiend**

In my childhood rumours ran
  Of a world beyond our door –
Terrors to the life of man
  That the highroad held in store.

Of the mermaids' doleful game
  In deep water I heard tell,
Or lofty dragons puffing flame,
  Or the hornèd fiend of Hell.

Tales like these were too absurd
  For my laughter-loving ear:
Soon I mocked at all I heard,
  Though with cause indeed for fear.

Now I know the mermaid kin
  I find them bound by natural laws:
They had neither tail nor fin,
  But are deadlier for that cause.

Dragons have no darting tongues,
  Teeth saw-edged nor rattling scales,
No fire issues from their lungs,
  No black poison from their tails:

For they are creatures of dark air,
  Unsubstantial tossing forms,
Thunderclaps of man's despair
  In mid-whirl of mental storms.

And there's a true and only fiend
  Worse than prophets prophesy,
Whose full powers to hurt are screened
  Lest the race of men should die.

Ever in vain will courage plot
  The dragon's death, in coat of proof;
Or love abjure the mermaid grot;
  Or faith denounce the cloven hoof.

Mermaids will not be denied
  The last bubbles of our shame,
The dragon flaunts an unpierced hide,
  The true fiend governs in God's name.

ROBERT GRAVES

321 **Piano**

Softly, in the dusk, a woman is singing to me;
Taking me back down the vista of years, till I see
A child sitting under the piano, in the boom of the
  tingling strings
And pressing the small, poised feet of a mother who
  smiles as she sings.

In spite of myself, the insidious mastery of song
Betrays me back, till the heart of me weeps to belong
To the old Sunday evenings at home, with winter
  outside
And hymns in the cosy parlour, the tinkling piano our
  guide.

So now it is vain for the singer to burst into clamour
With the great black piano apassionato. The glamour
Of childish days is upon me, my manhood is cast
Down in the flood of remembrance. I weep like a
  child for the past.

D. H. LAWRENCE

322 **Empty House**

Then, when the child was gone,
I was alone
In the house, suddenly grown vast. Each noise
Explained its origin away,
Animal, vegetable, mineral,
Nail, creaking board, or mouse.
But mostly there was quiet of after battle
Round the room where lay
The soldiers and the paintbox, all the toys,
  Then, when I went to tidy these away,
My hands refused to serve:
My body was the house,
And everything he'd touched, an exposed nerve.

STEPHEN SPENDER

323 **Solitude**

When you have tidied all things for the night,
And while your thoughts are fading to their sleep,
You'll pause a moment in the late firelight,
Too sorrowful to weep.

The large and gentle furniture has stood
In sympathetic silence all the day
With that old kindness of domestic wood;
Nevertheless the haunted room will say:
"Someone must be away."

The little dog rolls over half awake,
Stretches his paws, yawns, looking up at you,
Wags his tail very slightly for your sake,
That you may feel he is unhappy too.

A distant engine whistles, or the floor
Creaks, or the wandering night-wind bangs a door.

Silence is scattered like a broken glass.
The minutes prick their ears and run about,
Then one by one subside again and pass
Sedately in, monotonously out.

You bend your head and wipe away a tear.
Solitude walks one heavy step more near.

HAROLD MONRO

Now that the chill October day is declining,
Pull the blinds, draw each voluminous curtain,
Till the room is full of gloom and of the uncertain
Gleams of firelight on polished edges shining.
Then bring the rosy lamp to its wonted station
On the dark-gleaming table. In that soft splendour
Well-known things of the room, grown deep and
tender,
Gather round, a mysterious congregation:
Pallid sheen of the silver, the bright brass fender,
The wine-red pool of carpet, the bowl of roses,
Lustrous-hearted, crimsons and purples looming
From dusky rugs and curtains. Nothing discloses
The unseen walls, but the broken, richly-glooming
Gold of frames and opulent wells of mingling
Dim colours gathered in darkened mirrors. And
breaking
The dreamlike spell, and your deep chair forsaking,
You go, perhaps, to the shelves and, slowly singling
Some old rich-blazoned book, return. But the
gleaming
Spells close round you again and you fall to dreaming,
Eyes grown dim, the book on your lap unheeded.

MARTIN ARMSTRONG

325 **Hearthstone**

I want nothing but your fireside now.
Friend, you are sitting there alone I know,
And the quiet flames are licking up the soot,
Or crackling out of some enormous root:
All the logs on your hearth are four feet long.
Everything in your room is wide and strong
According to the breed of your hard thought.
Now you are leaning forward; you have caught
That great dog by his paw and are holding it,
And he looks sidelong at you, stretching a bit,
Drowsing with open eyes, huge, warm and wide,
The full hearth-length on his slow-breathing side.
Your book has dropped unnoticed: you have read
So long you cannot send your brain to bed.
The low quiet room and all its things are caught
And linger in the meshes of your thought.
(Some people think they know time cannot pause.)
Your eyes are closing now though not because
Of sleep. You are searching something with your
brain;
You have let the old dog's paw drop down again . . .
Now suddenly you hum a little catch,
And pick up the book. The wind rattles the latch;
There's a patter of light cool rain and the curtain shakes;
The silly dog growls, moves, and almost wakes.
The kettle near the fire one moment hums.
Then a long peace upon the whole room comes.
So the sweet evening will draw to its bedtime end.
I want nothing but your fireside, friend.

HAROLD MONRO

326 **The Listeners**

"Is there anybody there?" said the Traveller,
  Knocking on the moonlit door;
And his horse in the silence champed the grasses
  Of the forest's ferny floor:
And a bird flew up out of the turret,
  Above the Traveller's head:
And he smote upon the door again a second time;
  "Is there anybody there?" he said.

But no one descended to the Traveller;
  No head from the leaf-fringed sill
Leaned over and looked into his grey eyes,
  Where he stood perplexed and still.
But only a host of phantom listeners
  That dwelt in the lone house then
Stood listening in the quiet of the moonlight
  To that voice from the world of men:
Stood thronging the faint moonbeams on the dark
    stair,
  That goes down to the empty hall,
Hearkening in an air stirred and shaken
  By the lonely Traveller's call.

And he felt in his heart their strangeness,
  Their stillness answering his cry,
While his horse moved, cropping the dark turf,
  'Neath the starred and leafy sky;
For he suddenly smote on the door, even
  Louder, and lifted his head: –
"Tell them I came, and no one answered,
  That I kept my word," he said.

Never the least stir made the listeners,
  Though every word he spake
Fell echoing through the shadowiness of the still house
  From the one man left awake:
Ay, they heard his foot upon the stirrup,
  And the sound of iron on stone,
And how the silence surged softly backward,
  When the plunging hoofs were gone.

WALTER DE LA MARE

327 The Old Stone House

Nothing on the grey roof, nothing on the brown,
Only a little greening where the rain drips down;
Nobody at the window, nobody at the door,
Only a little hollow which a foot once wore;
But still I tread on tiptoe, still tiptoe on I go,
Past nettles, porch, and weedy well, for oh, I know
A friendless face is peering, and a still clear eye
Peeps closely through the casement as my step goes by.

WALTER DE LA MARE

328 **Nobody Comes**

Tree-leaves labour up and down,
 And through them the fainting light
 Succumbs to the crawl of night.
Outside in the road the telegraph wire
 To the town from the darkening land
Intones to travellers like a spectral lyre
 Swept by a spectral hand.

A car comes up, with lamps full-glare,
 That flash upon a tree:
 It has nothing to do with me,
And whangs along in a world of its own,
 Leaving a blacker air;
And mute by the gate I stand again alone,
 And nobody pulls up there.

THOMAS HARDY

329 **The Lake Isle of Innisfree**

I will arise and go now, and go to Innisfree,
And a small cabin build there, of clay and wattles
  made;
Nine bean rows will I have there, a hive for the honey
  bee,
And live alone in the bee-loud glade.

And I shall have some peace there, for peace comes
  dropping slow,
Dropping from the veils of the morning to where the
  cricket sings;
There midnight's all a-glimmer, and noon a purple
  glow,
And evening full of the linnet's wings.

I will arise and go now, for always night and day
I hear lake water lapping with low sounds by the
  shore;
While I stand on the roadway, or on the pavements
  gray,
I hear it in the deep heart's core.

W. B. YEATS

330 **Growing Old**

What is it to grow old?
Is it to lose the glory of the form,
The lustre of the eye?
Is it for Beauty to forego her wreath?
Yes! but not this alone.

Is it to feel our strength –
Not our bloom only, but our strength – decay?
Is it to feel each limb
Grow stiffer, every function less exact,
Each nerve more weakly strung?

Yes! this, and more; but not,
Ah, 'tis not what in youth we dreamed 'twould be:
'Tis not to have our life
Mellowed and softened as with sunset-glow,
A golden day's decline.

'Tis not to see the world
As from a height, with rapt prophetic eyes
And heart profoundly stirred;
And weep, and feel the fulness of the past,
The years that are no more.

It is to spend long days
And not once feel that we were ever young;
It is to add, immured
In the hot prison of the present, month
To month with weary pain.

It is to suffer this,
And feel but half and feebly, what we feel.
Deep in our hidden heart
Festers the dull remembrance of a change,
But no emotion – none.

It is – last stage of all –
When we are frozen up within, and quite
The phantom of ourselves,
To hear the world applaud the hollow ghost
Which blamed the living man.

MATTHEW ARNOLD

331 **To Night**

Swiftly walk o'er the western wave,
 Spirit of Night!
Out of the misty eastern cave, –
 Where, all the long and lone daylight,
Thou wovest dreams of joy and fear
Which make thee terrible and dear, –
 Swift be thy flight!

Wrap thy form in a mantle grey,
  Star-inwrought!
Blind with thine hair the eyes of Day;
  Kiss her until she be wearied out.
Then wander o'er city and sea and land,
Touching all with thine opiate wand –
  Come, long-sought!

When I arose and saw the dawn,
  I sighed for thee;
When light rode high, and the dew was gone,
  And noon lay heavy on flower and tree,
And the weary Day turned to his rest,
Lingering like an unloved guest,
  I sighed for thee.

Thy brother Death came, and cried,
  "Wouldst thou me?"
Thy sweet child Sleep, the filmy-eyed,
  Murmured like a noontide bee,
"Shall I nestle near thy side?
Wouldst thou me?" – And I replied,
  "No, not thee!"

Death will come when thou art dead,
  Soon, too soon –
Sleep will come when thou art fled,
  Of neither would I ask the boon
I ask of thee, belovèd Night –
Swift be thine approaching flight,
  Come soon, soon!

PERCY BYSSHE SHELLEY

332 To Sleep

A flock of sheep that leisurely pass by,
One after one; the sound of rain, and bees
Murmuring; the fall of rivers, winds and seas,
Smooth fields, white sheets of water, and pure sky;
I have thought of all by turns, and yet to lie
Sleepless! and soon the small birds' melodies
Must hear, first uttered from my orchard trees;
And the first cuckoo's melancholy cry.
Even thus last night, and two nights more, I lay
And could not win thee, Sleep! by any stealth:
So do not let me wear to-night away:
Without thee what is all the morning's wealth?
Come, blessed barrier between day and day,
Dear mother of fresh thoughts and joyous health!

WILLIAM WORDSWORTH

333 To Sleep

O soft embalmer of the still midnight!
  Shutting with careful fingers and benign
Our gloom-pleased eyes, embowered from the light,
  Enshaded in forgetfulness divine;
O soothest Sleep! if so it please thee, close,
  In midst of this thine hymn, my willing eyes,
Or wait the amen, ere thy poppy throws
  Around my bed its lulling charities;
  Then save me, or the passèd day will shine
Upon my pillow, breeding many woes;
Save me from curious conscience, that still lords
  Its strength for darkness, burrowing like a mole;
Turn the key deftly in the oilèd wards,
  And seal the hushèd casket of my soul.

JOHN KEATS

334 **Falling Asleep**

Voices moving about in the quiet house:
Thud of feet and a muffled shutting of doors:
Everyone yawning. Only the clocks are alert.

Out in the night there's autumn-smelling gloom
Crowded with whispering trees; across the park
A hollow cry of hounds like lonely bells:
And I know that the clouds are moving across the
  moon;
The low, red, rising moon. Now herons call
And wrangle by their pool; and hooting owls
Sail from the wood above pale stooks of oats.

Waiting for sleep, I drift from thoughts like these;
And where to-day was dream-like, build my dreams.
Music . . . there was a bright white room below,
And someone singing a song about a soldier,
One hour, two hours ago: and soon the song
Will be "*last night*": but now the beauty swings
Across my brain, ghost of remembered chords
Which still can make such radiance in my dream
That I can watch the marching of my soldiers,
And count their faces; faces; sunlit faces.

Falling asleep . . . the herons, and the hounds . . .
September in the darkness; and the world
I've known; all fading past me into peace.

SIEGFRIED SASSOON

335 The Last Word

Creep into thy narrow bed,
Creep, and let no more be said!
Vain thy onset! all stands fast.
Thou thyself must break at last.

Let the long contention cease!
Geese are swans, and swans are geese.
Let them have it how they will!
Thou art tired; best be still.

They out-talked thee, hissed thee, tore thee?
Better men fared thus before thee;
Fired their ringing shot and passed
Hotly charged – and sank at last.

Charge once more, then, and be dumb!
Let the victors, when they come,
When the forts of folly fall,
Find thy body by the wall!

MATTHEW ARNOLD

Poetry . . . is the attempt to imagine, in terms of the transitory forms of the present in which a generation lives, the universal nature of man's being.

Stephen Spender

336 Like to the Grass

Like to the grass that's newly sprung,
Or like a tale that's new begun,
Or like the bird that's here to-day,
Or like the pearlèd dew of May,
Or like an hour, or like a span,
Or like the singing of a swan –
Even such is man, who lives by breath,
Is here, now there: so life, and death.
The grass withers, the tale is ended,
The bird is flown, the dew's ascended,
The hour is short, the span not long,
The swan's near death; man's life is done.

Like to the bubble in the brook,
Or, in a glass, much like a look,
Or like a shuttle in weaver's hand,
Or like writing on the sand,
Or like a thought, or like a dream,
Or like the gliding of the stream –
Even such is man, who lives by breath,
Is here, now there: so life, and death.
The bubble's cut, the look's forgot,
The shuttle's flung, the writing's blot,
The thought is past, the dream is gone,
The water glides; man's life is done.

ANONYMOUS

337 Love's Secret

Never seek to tell thy love,
   Love that never told can be;
For the gentle wind doth move
   Silently, invisibly.

I told my love, I told my love,
   I told her all my heart,
Trembling, cold, in ghastly fears,
   Ah! she did depart!

Soon after she was gone from me,
   A traveller came by,
Silently, invisibly:
   He took her with a sigh.

WILLIAM BLAKE

338 **Bredon Hill**

In summertime on Bredon
  The bells they sound so clear;
Round both the shires they ring them
  In steeples far and near,
  A happy noise to hear.

Here of a Sunday morning
  My love and I would lie,
And see the coloured counties,
  And hear the larks so high
  About us in the sky.

The bells would ring to call her
  In valleys miles away:
"Come all to church, good people;
  Good people, come and pray."
  But here my love would stay.

And I would turn and answer
  Among the springing thyme,
"Oh, peal upon our wedding,
  And we will hear the chime,
  And come to church in time."

But when the snows at Christmas
  On Bredon top were strown,
My love rose up so early
  And stole out unbeknown
  And went to church alone.

They tolled the one bell only,
  Groom there was none to see,
The mourners followed after,
  And so to church went she,
  And would not wait for me.

The bells they sound on Bredon,
  And still the steeples hum
"Come all to church, good people,"
  Oh, noisy bells, be dumb;
  I hear you, I will come.

A. E. HOUSMAN

339 **The Death of Ophelia** (From *Hamlet*)

There is a willow grows aslant a brook,
That shows his hoar leaves in the glassy stream;
There with fantastic garlands did she come,
Of crow-flowers, nettles, daisies and long purples,
That liberal shepherds give a grosser name,
But our cold maids do dead men's fingers call them.
There, on the pendent boughs her coronet weeds
Clambering to hang, an envious sliver broke,
When down her weedy trophies and herself
Fell in the weeping brook. Her clothes spread wide,
And, mermaid-like, awhile they bore her up;
Which time she chanted snatches of old tunes,
As one incapable of her own distress,
Or like a creature native and indued
Unto that element: but long it could not be
Till that her garments, heavy with their drink,
Pulled the poor wretch from her melodious lay
To muddy death.

WILLIAM SHAKESPEARE

340 **Song**

When I am dead, my dearest,
  Sing no sad songs for me;
Plant thou no roses at my head,
  Nor shady cypress tree:
Be the green grass above me
  With showers and dewdrops wet;
And if thou wilt, remember,
  And if thou wilt, forget.

I shall not see the shadows,
  I shall not feel the rain;
I shall not hear the nightingale
  Sing on as if in pain:
And dreaming through the twilight
  That doth not rise nor set,
Haply I may remember,
  And haply may forget.

CHRISTINA ROSSETTI

341 **Weep You No More**

Weep you no more, sad fountains;
  What need you flow so fast?
Look how the snowy mountains
  Heaven's sun doth gently waste!
But my Sun's heavenly eyes
  View not your weeping,
  That now lies sleeping
Softly, now softly lies
  Sleeping.

Sleep is a reconciling,
  A rest that peace begets:
Doth not the sun rise smiling
  When fair at ev'n he sets?
Rest you then, rest, sad eyes!
  Melt not in weeping,
  While she lies sleeping
Softly, now softly lies
  Sleeping.

ANONYMOUS

342 **A Dirge**

Why were you born when the snow was falling?
You should have come to the cuckoo's calling,
Or when grapes are green in the cluster,
Or, at least, when lithe swallows muster
  For their far off flying
  From summer dying.

Why did you die when the lambs were cropping?
You should have died at the apples' dropping,
When the grasshopper comes to trouble,
And the wheat-fields are sodden stubble,
  And all winds go sighing
  For sweet things dying.

CHRISTINA ROSSETTI

343 **Seascape**

In Memoriam, M.A.S.

There are some days the happy ocean lies
Like an unfingered harp, below the land.
Afternoon gilds all the silent wires
Into a burning music for the eyes.
On mirrors flashing between fine-strung fires
The shore, heaped up with roses, horses, spires,
Wanders on water, walking above ribbed sand.

The motionlessness of the hot sky tires
And a sigh, like a woman's, from inland
Brushes the instrument with shadowing hand
Drawing across its wires some gull's sharp cries
Or bell, or shout, from distant, hedged-in shires;
These, deep as anchors, the hushing wave buries.

Then from the shore, two zig-zag butterflies,
Like errant dog-roses, cross the bright strand
Spiralling over sea in foolish gyres
Until they fall into reflected skies.
They drown. Fishermen understand
Such wings sunk in such ritual sacrifice,

Recalling legends of undersea, drowned cities.
What voyagers, oh what heroes, flamed like pyres
With helmets plumed, have set forth from some island
And them the sea engulfed. Their eyes,
Contorted by the cruel waves' desires
Glitter with coins through the tide scarcely scanned,
While, above them, that harp assumes their sighs.

STEPHEN SPENDER

344 A Lamentation

All looks be pale, hearts cold as stone,
For Hally now is dead and gone.
  Hally in whose sight,
    Most sweet sight,
All the earth late took delight.
  Every eye, weep with me,
  Joys drowned in tears must be.

His ivory skin, his comely hair,
His rosy cheeks so clear and fair,
  Eyes that once did grace
    His bright face,
Now in him all want their place.
  Eyes and hearts, weep with me,
  For who so kind as he?

His youth was like an April flower,
Adorned with beauty, love, and power.
  Glory strewed his way,
    Whose wreaths gay
Now all are turnèd to decay.
  Then, again, weep with me,
  None feel more cause than we.

No more may his wishèd sight return.
His golden lamp no more can burn.
  Quenched is all his flame.
    His hoped fame

Now hath left him nought but name.
  For him all weep with me,
  Since more him none shall see.

THOMAS CAMPION

345 **Lament** (From *Cymbeline*)

Fear no more the heat o' the sun,
  Nor the furious winter's rages;
Thou thy worldly task hast done,
  Home art gone, and ta'en thy wages.
Golden lads and girls all must,
As chimney-sweepers, come to dust.

Fear no more the frown o' the great,
  Thou art past the tyrant's stroke;
Care no more to clothe and eat;
  To thee the reed is as the oak.
The sceptre, learning, physic must
All follow this, and come to dust.

Fear no more the lightning-flash,
  Nor the all-dreaded thunder-stone;
Fear not slander, censure rash;
  Thou hast finished joy and moan.
All lovers young, all lovers must
Consign to thee, and come to dust.

No exorciser harm thee!
Nor no witchcraft charm thee!
Ghost unlaid forbear thee!
Nothing ill come near thee!
Quiet consummation have,
And renownèd be thy grave!

WILLIAM SHAKESPEARE

346 The Author's Epitaph

Even such is Time, that takes in trust
  Our youth, our joys, our all we have,
And pays us but with age and dust;
  Who in the dark and silent grave,
When we have wandered all our ways,
Shuts up the story of our days;
But from this earth, this grave, this dust,
My God shall raise me up, I trust.

WALTER RALEIGH

347 Death, Be Not Proud

Death, be not proud, though some have callèd thee
Mighty and dreadful, for thou art not so:
For those whom thou think'st thou dost overthrow
Die not, poor Death; nor yet canst thou kill me.
From rest and sleep, which but thy pictures be,
Much pleasure, then from thee much more must flow;
And soonest our best men with thee do go –
Rest of their bones, and souls' delivery!
Thou art slave to fate, chance, kings, and desperate
men,
And dost with poison, war, and sickness dwell;
And poppy or charms can make us sleep as well
And better than thy stroke. Why swell'st thou then?
One short sleep past, we wake eternally,
And death shall be no more: Death, thou shalt die!

JOHN DONNE

348 **Afterwards**

When the Present has latched its postern behind
  my tremulous stay,
And the May month flaps its glad green leaves
  like wings,
Delicate-filmed as new-spun silk, will the neighbours
  say,
"He was a man who used to notice such things"?

If it be in the dusk when, like an eyelid's soundless
  blink,
The dewfall-hawk comes crossing the shades to alight
Upon the wind-warped upland thorn, a gazer may think,
"To him this must have been a familiar sight."

If I pass during some nocturnal blackness, mothy and
warm,
When the hedgehog travels furtively over the lawn,
One may say, "He strove that such innocent creatures
should come to no harm,
But he could do little for them; and now he is gone."

If, when hearing that I have been stilled at last,
they stand at the door,
Watching the full-starred heavens that winter sees,
Will this thought rise on those who will meet my face
no more,
"He was one who had an eye for such mysteries"?

And will any say when my bell of quittance is heard
in the gloom,
And a crossing breeze cuts a pause in its outrollings,
Till they rise again, as they were a new bell's boom,
"He hears it not now, but used to notice such
things"?

THOMAS HARDY

INDEX OF AUTHORS

INDEX OF FIRST LINES

ACKNOWLEDGMENTS

For permission to include copyright material in this anthology the compiler and publishers wish to make the following acknowledgments: "Enchantment" by Æ is reprinted by permission of Diarmuid Russell and A. M. Heath & Co. Ltd; "Mrs. Reece Laughs" and "In Lamplight" by Martin Armstrong by permission of A. D. Peters & Co.; "On This Island", "Night Mail", "O What Is That Sound?" and "Who's Who" by W. H. Auden, from *Collected Shorter Poems 1927–1957*, by permission of Faber and Faber Ltd; "I Had a Hippopotamus" by Patrick Barrington by permission of *Punch*; "Matilda" and "The Frog" by Hilaire Belloc by permission of Gerald Duckworth & Co. Ltd; "Tarantella" by Hilaire Belloc by permission of A. D. Peters & Co.; "Flame and Snow" and "The Belfry" by Laurence Binyon by permission of the Society of Authors as the literary representative of the estate of the late Laurence Binyon; "Midnight Skaters", "The Poor Man's Pig" and "Thames Gulls" by Edmund Blunden by permission of A. D. Peters & Co.; "As I Came Home from Labour" by F. C. Boden, from *Out of the Coalfields*, by permission of J. M. Dent & Sons Ltd; "Spring Goeth All in White", "North Wind in October", "November", "London Snow", "I Heard a Linnet Courting", "A Passer-By", "I Love All Beauteous Things" and "Triolet" by Robert Bridges by permission of the Clarendon Press, Oxford; "King's College Chapel", from *Union Street* (Hart-Davis), and "By St Thomas Water" (published in *The Listener*) by Charles Causley by permission of David Higham Associates Ltd; "Cambridgeshire" by Frances Cornford, from *Collected Poems*, by permission of The Cresset Press; "Trees", "Silver", "The Linnet", "Music", "Fare Well", "Goliath", "The Listeners" and "The Old Stone House" by Walter de la Mare by permission of the literary trustees of Walter de la Mare and the Society of Authors as their representative; "The Winter Trees" and "The Snow" by Clifford Dyment, from *Poems 1935–1948*, by permission of J. M. Dent & Sons Ltd; "Journey of the Magi" by T. S. Eliot, from *Collected Poems 1909–1962*, "Macavity: The Mystery Cat" and "Gus: The Theatre Cat" by T. S. Eliot, from *Old Possum's Book of Practical Cats*, by permission of Faber & Faber Ltd; "Mending Wall", "The Line-Gang", "Good-Bye and Keep Cold", "The Road Not Taken" and "Acquainted with the Night" by Robert Frost, from *The Complete Poems of Robert Frost*, by permission of Laurence Pollinger Ltd, Jonathan Cape Ltd and the proprietors Holt, Rinehart and Winston, Inc.; "The End of a Leave" and "The Bay" by Roy Fuller, from *Collected Poems*, by permission of André Deutsch Ltd; "Above the Storm" by W. W. Gibson, from *Islands: Poems 1930–1932*, by permission of Mr Michael Gibson and Macmillan & Co. Ltd; "Flying Crooked", "The Beach", "The Visitation", "The Straw" and "A Slice of Wedding Cake", from *Collected Poems 1965*, "Here Live Your Life Out!", from *More Poems 1961*, and "Mermaid, Dragon, Fiend", from *Collected Poems 1959*, by Robert Graves by permission of the author and A. P. Watt & Son; "Apartment Cats" by Thom Gunn (published in *The Listener*) by permission of the author; "April Day: Binsey" and "London Tom-Cat" by Michael Hamburger by permission of the author; "Spring Song in Winter" by Michael Hamburger, from *Dual Site*, by permission of Michael Hamburger; "Snow in the Suburbs", "Throwing a Tree: New Forest", "Weathers", "The Oxen", "A Thunderstorm in Town", "Drummer Hodge", "Waiting Both", "At a Lunar Eclipse", "Nobody Comes" and "Afterwards" by Thomas Hardy, from *The Collected Poems of Thomas Hardy*, by permission of the trustees of the Hardy Estate, The Macmillan Company of Canada Ltd and Macmillan & Co. Ltd, London; "The Bells of Heaven" and "Stupidity Street" by Ralph Hodgson, from *The*

Collected Poems of Ralph Hodgson, by permission of Mrs Hodgson, Macmillan & Co. Ltd, London and the Macmillan Company of Canada Ltd; "Pied Beauty" and "Spring" by Gerard Manley Hopkins, from *The Poems of Gerard Manley Hopkins*, by courtesy of Oxford University Press; "Loveliest of Trees", "When I Would Muse in Boyhood" and "Bredon Hill" by A. E. Housman by permission of the Society of Authors as the literary representative of the estate of the late A. E. Housman, and Jonathan Cape Ltd, publishers of A. E. Housman's *Collected Poems*; "Wind", from *The Hawk in the Rain*, and "November", "View of a Pig" and "An Otter", from *Lupercal*, by Ted Hughes by permission of Faber & Faber Ltd; "The Way Through the Woods" and "If—" by Rudyard Kipling, from *Rewards and Fairies*, by permission of Mrs George Bambridge, Macmillan & Co. Ltd and A. P. Watt & Son; "Summer Night", "The Lakeside, Corsham" and "The Astronaut" by James Kirkup, from *The Prodigal Son*, by permission of the author; "At Grass" by Philip Larkin, from *The Less Deceived*, by permission of The Marvell Press, England: "Kangaroo", "Snake", "Bat", "Letter from Town: The Almond-Tree", "Baby Running Barefoot" and "Piano" by D. H. Lawrence, from *The Complete Poems of D. H. Lawrence*, by permission of William Heinemann Ltd, Laurence Pollinger Ltd and the estate of the late Mrs Frieda Lawrence; "April Rise", "Day of These Days", "Field of Autumn", "Town Owl" and "Sunken Evening" by Laurie Lee by permission of André Deutsch Ltd; "All Day It Has Rained" by Alun Lewis, from *Raiders' Dawn*, by permission of George Allen & Unwin Ltd; "Now the Full-Throated Daffodils", "Windy Day in August", "A Hard Frost", "Sheepdog Trials in Hyde Park", "The Ecstatic", "Seen from the Train", "The Album", "Come, Live with Me and Be My Love", "Will It Be So Again?" and "A Carol" by C. Day Lewis, from *Collected Poems 1954*, by permission of the Hogarth Press and Jonathan Cape Ltd; "Aubade" and "Losing a Sail" by Edward Lucie-Smith, from *A Tropical Childhood*, by permission of Oxford University Press; "Feeding Ducks" by Norman MacCaig, from *A Common Grace*, by permission of The Hogarth Press; "Sleeping Compartment" by Norman MacCaig (published in *The Listener*) by permission of the author; "The Cyclist" and "Prayer before Birth" by Louis MacNeice, from *Collected Poems*, by permission of Faber & Faber Ltd; "Tewkesbury Road" and "Sea Fever" by John Masefield by permission of the Society of Authors as the literary representative of the estate of John Masefield; "The Girl's Confession" by Eric Millward (published in *The Listener*) by permission of the author; "Milk for the Cat", "The Nightingale near the House", "Solitude" and "Hearthstone" by Harold Monro by permission of Mrs A. Monro; "The Animals" and "The Castle" by Edwin Muir, from *Collected Poems*, by permission of Faber & Faber Ltd; "Adventures of Isabel" and "What's the Use?" by Ogden Nash, from *The Face is Familiar*, by permission of J. M. Dent & Sons Ltd: "Last Leaves" and "Curlew" by Leslie Norris, from *Finding the Gold*, by permission of Chatto & Windus Ltd; "From My Diary, July 1914", "Anthem for Doomed Youth", "The Send-Off", "Strange Meeting" and "Futility" by Wilfred Owen, from *The Collected Poems of Wilfred Owen*, by permission of Mr Harold and Chatto & Windus Ltd; "Travelling Between Places" by Brian Patten (published in *The Listener*), from *Little Johnny's Confession*, by permission of George Allen & Unwin Ltd; "Mushrooms" by Sylvia Plath by permission of Miss Olwyn Hughes; "Naming of Parts" by Henry Reed, from *A Map of Verona*, by permission of Jonathan Cape Ltd; "The Birds" by Clive Sansom by permission of *Punch*; "Morning Express", "A Local Train of Thought", "In the Pink" and "Falling Asleep" by Siegfried Sassoon by permission of the author; "Moods of Rain" by Vernon Scannell (published in *The Listener*) by permission of the author; "The Rock Pool" and "Boats at Night" by Edward Shanks, from *Poems 1912–1932*, by permission of Mrs Shanks and Macmillan & Co. Ltd; "Winter, the Hunstman" by Osbert Sitwell by permission of Gerald Duckworth & Co. Ltd; "By Ferry to the Island" by Iain

Crichton Smith, from *Thistles and Roses*, by permission of Eyre & Spottiswoode Ltd; "The Pylons", "The Express", "How Strangely This Sun", "I Think Continually", "Children Who Were Rough", "Empty House" and "Seascape" by Stephen Spender, from *Collected Poems*, by permission of Faber & Faber Ltd; "Late Snow" and "The Discovery" by J. C. Squire, from *Collected Poems*, by permission of Mr Raglan Squire, the Macmillan Company of Canada Ltd and Macmillan & Co. Ltd, London; "A Peasant", from *Song at the Year's Turning*, and "A Blackbird Singing", from *Poetry for Supper*, by R. S. Thomas by permission of Rupert Hart-Davis Ltd; "Hedgehog" and "Disturbances" by Anthony Thwaite, from *The Owl in the Tree*, by permission of Oxford University Press; "War Poem" and "Conquerors" by Henry Treece, from *The Black Seasons*, by permission of Faber & Faber Ltd; "Au Jardin des Plantes" by John Wain by permission of Routledge & Kegan Paul Ltd; "Lapwing" and "Chough" by R. E. Warner, from *Poems and Contradictions*, by permission of The Bodley Head; "The Feather", from *The Lady with the Unicorn*, and "The Heron", from *The Death Bell*, by Vernon Watkins by permission of Faber & Faber Ltd; "The Wild Swans at Coole", "The Fiddler of Dooney", "The Cloths of Heaven", "When You Are Old", "Down by the Salley Gardens", "The Cap and Bells", "An Irish Airman Foresees His Death", "To a Friend Whose Work Has Come to Nothing" and "The Lake Isle of Innisfree" by W. B. Yeats, from *Collected Poems of W. B. Yeats*, by permission of Mr M. B. Yeats, Macmillan & Co. Ltd and A. P. Watt and Son; "Last Snow", from *The Collected Poems of Andrew Young*, and "Cuckoos", "The Swallows" and "The Echoing Cliff", from *Quiet as Moss*, by Andrew Young by permission of Rupert Hart-Davis Ltd.

Copyright portraits are reproduced by permission of the National Portrait Gallery, London.